DON CASTILLO'S
MOST SEXIEST
Women Art!

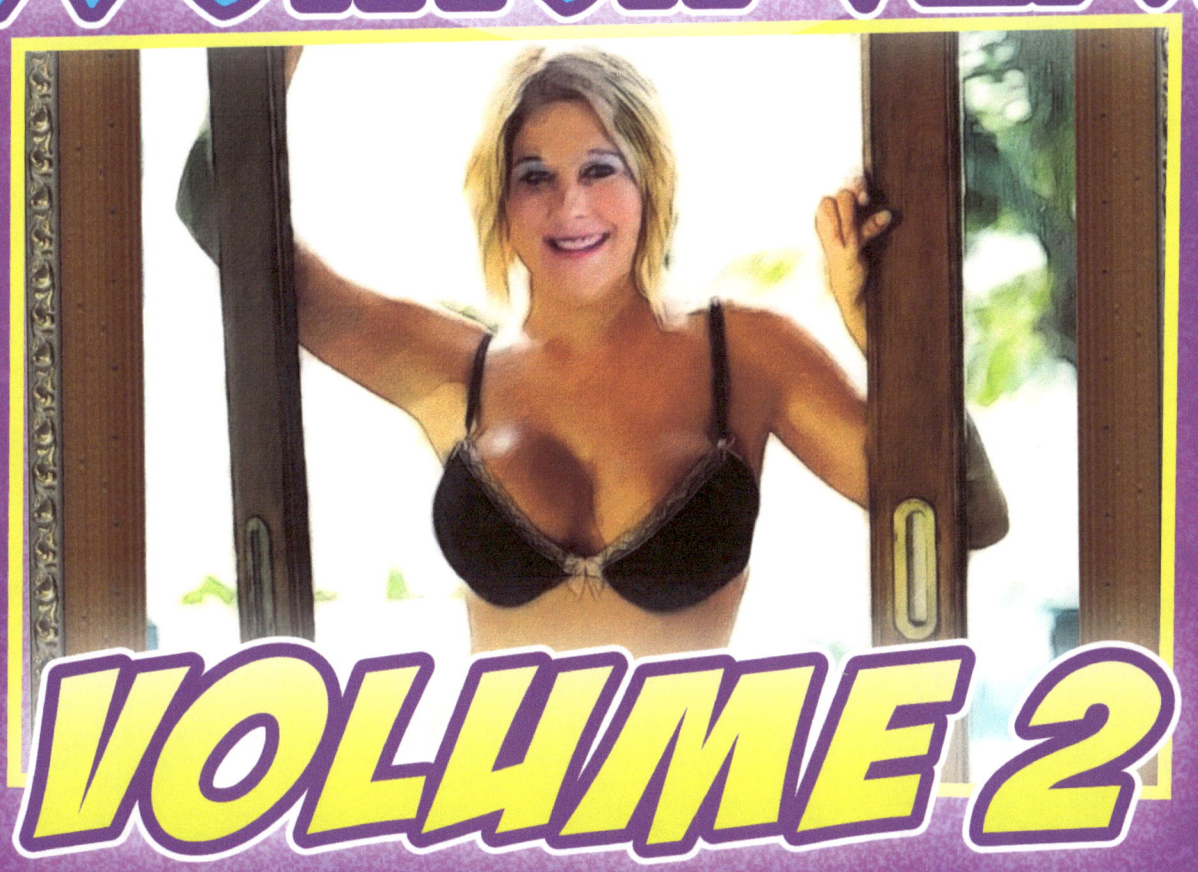

VOLUME 2

DEDICATION:

THANKS TO EVERYONE FOR BUYING THIS BOOK AND ALL THE LOVE AND SUPPORT I GET FROM MY FAMILY AND FRIENDS.
WRITE ME AT DONLEEJKD@AOL.COM OR FIND ME AT DON CASTILLO ON FACEBOOK.COM

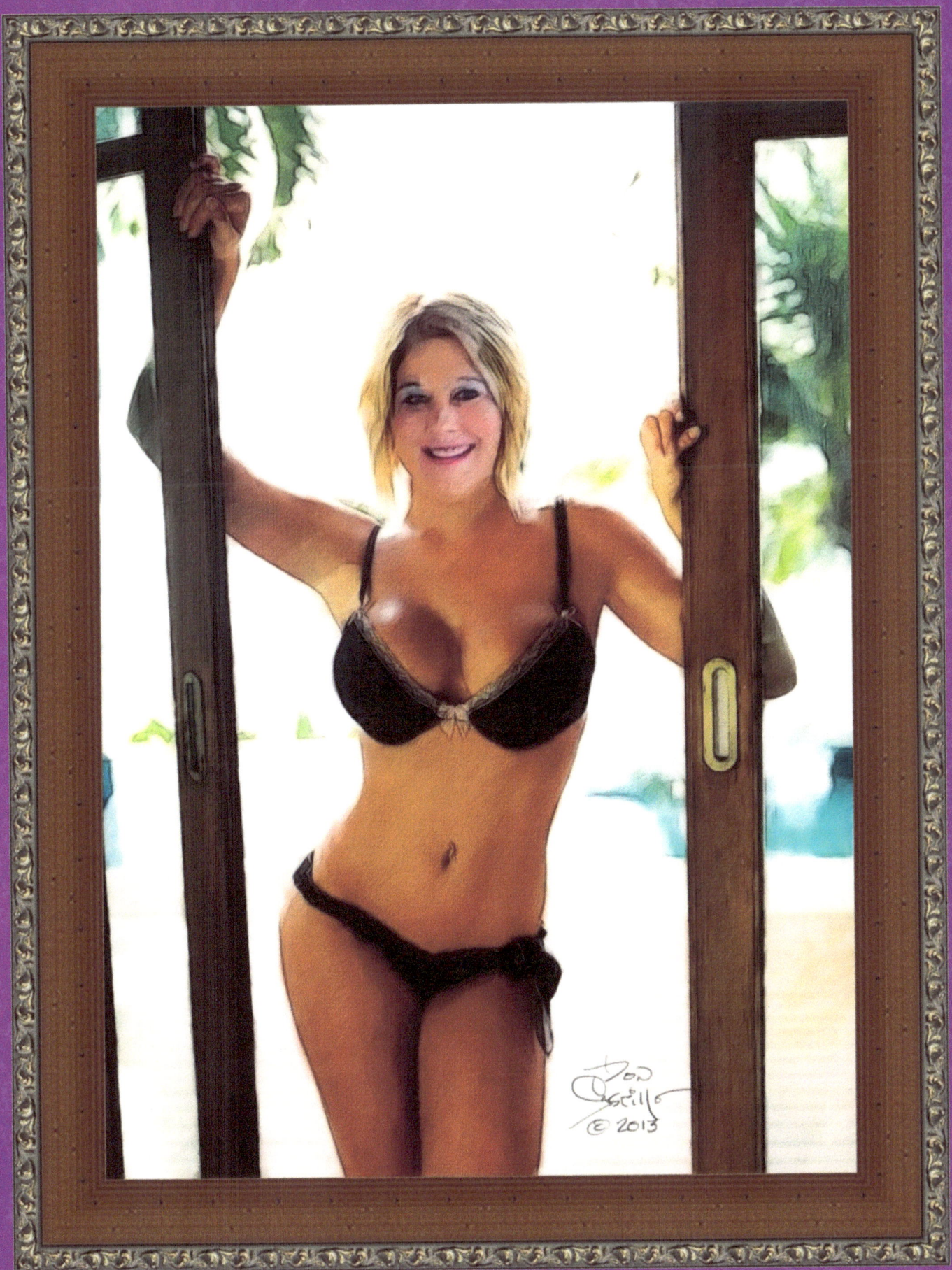

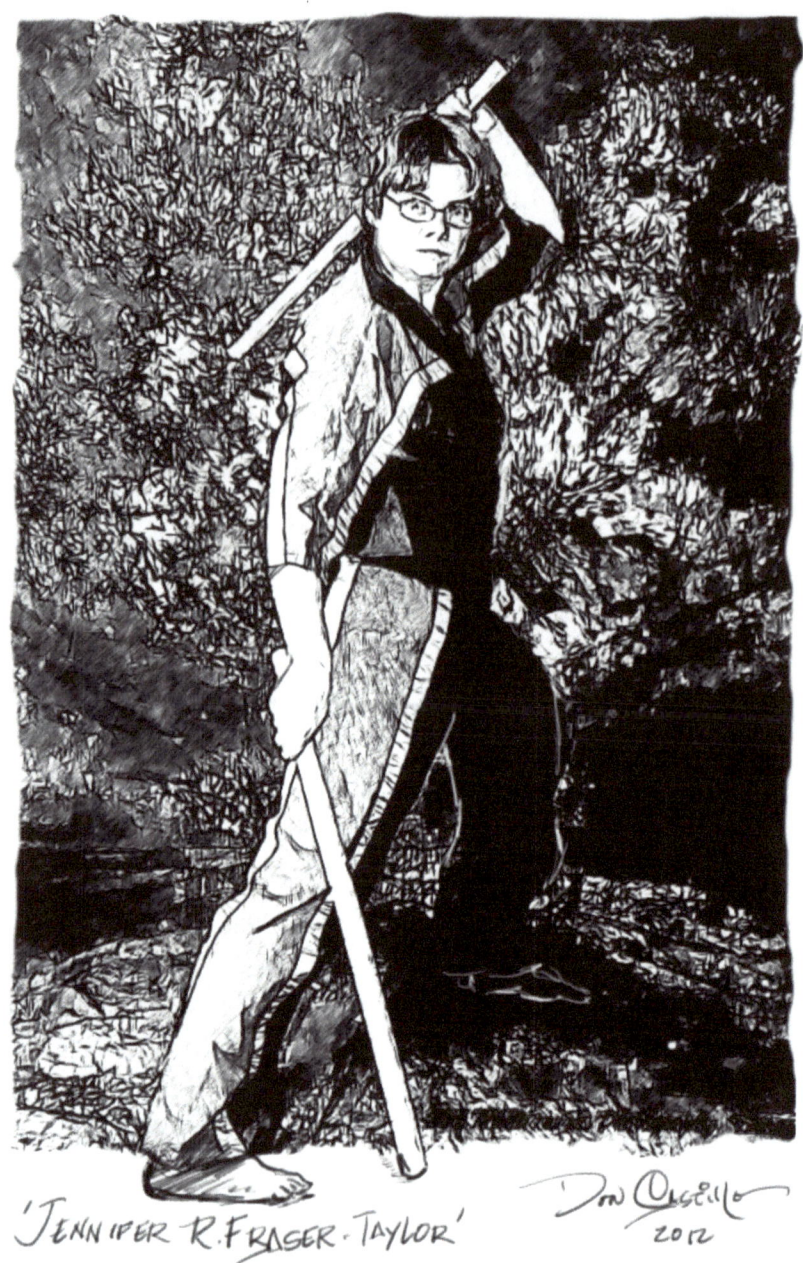

'JENNIFER R. FRASER · TAYLOR'

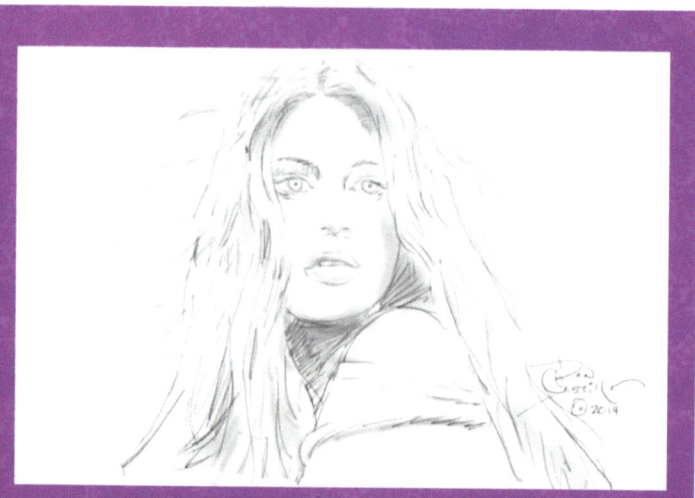

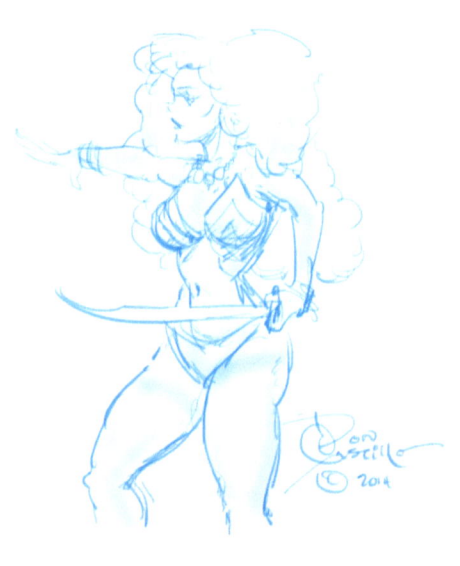

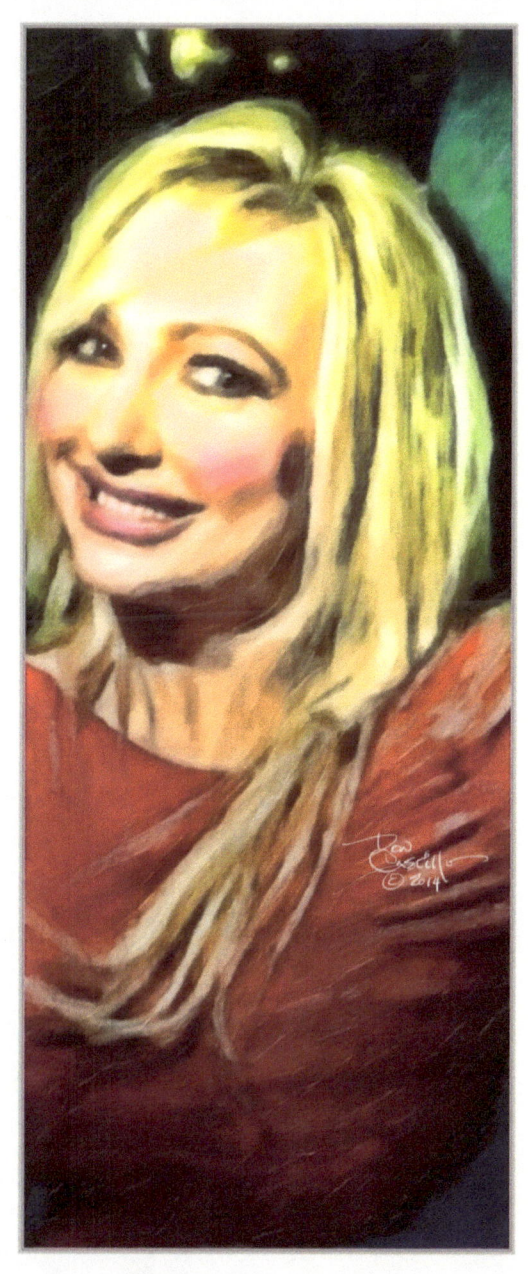

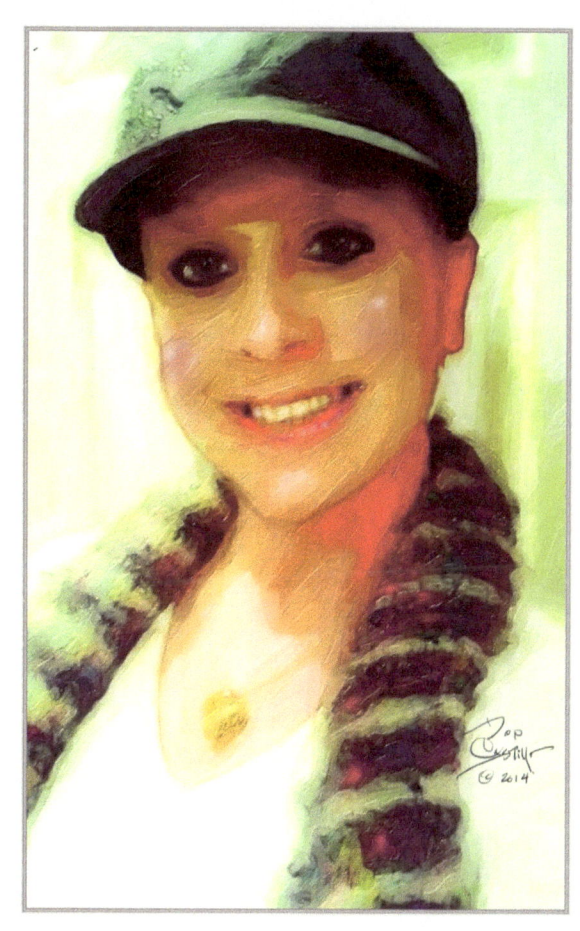

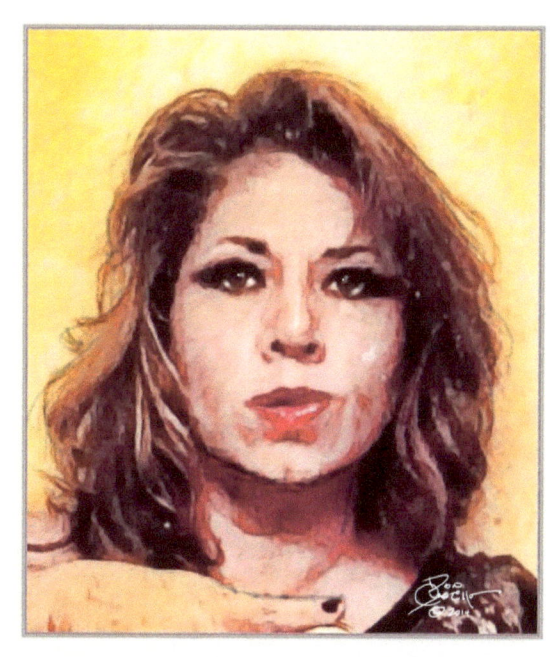

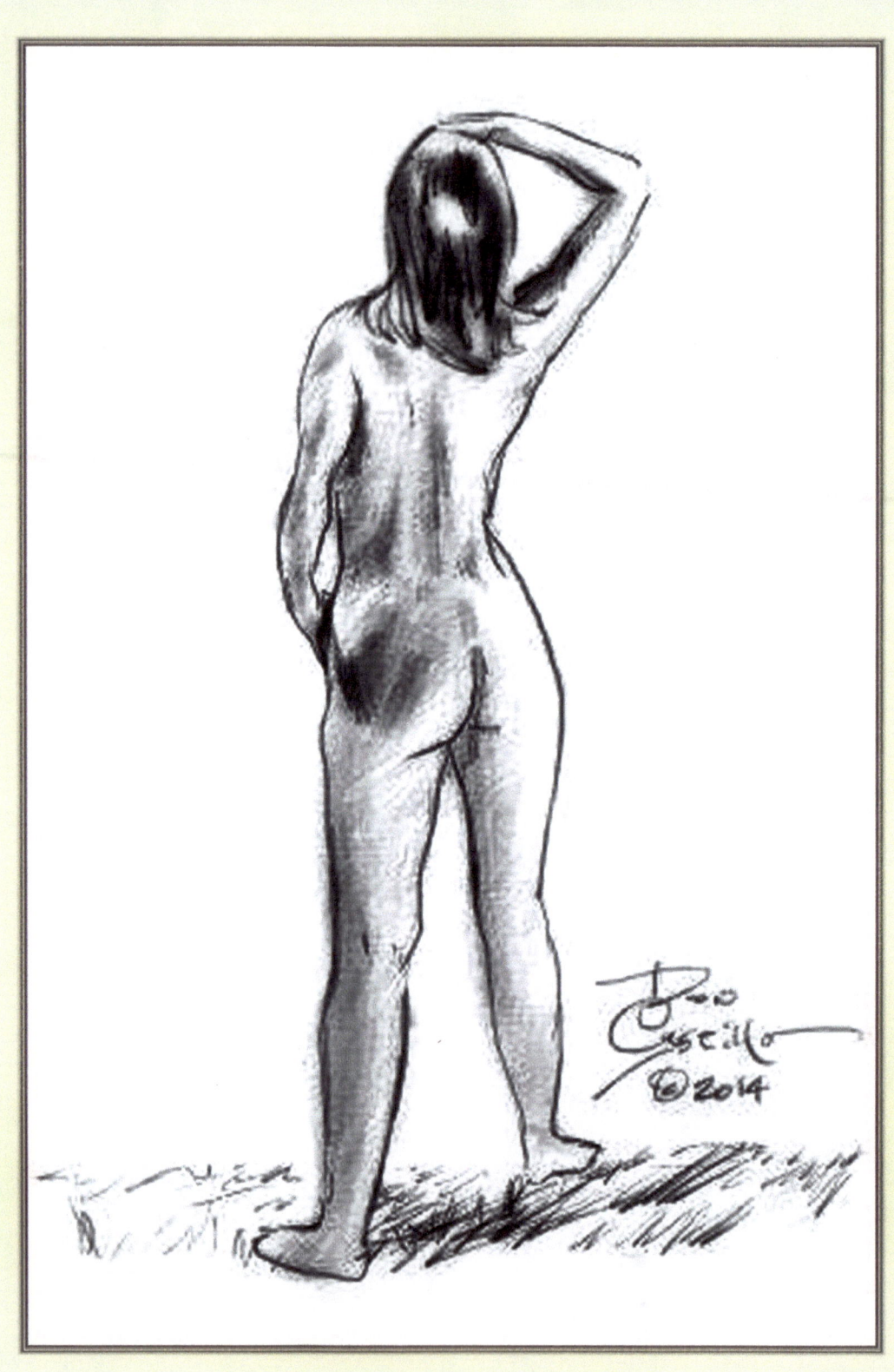

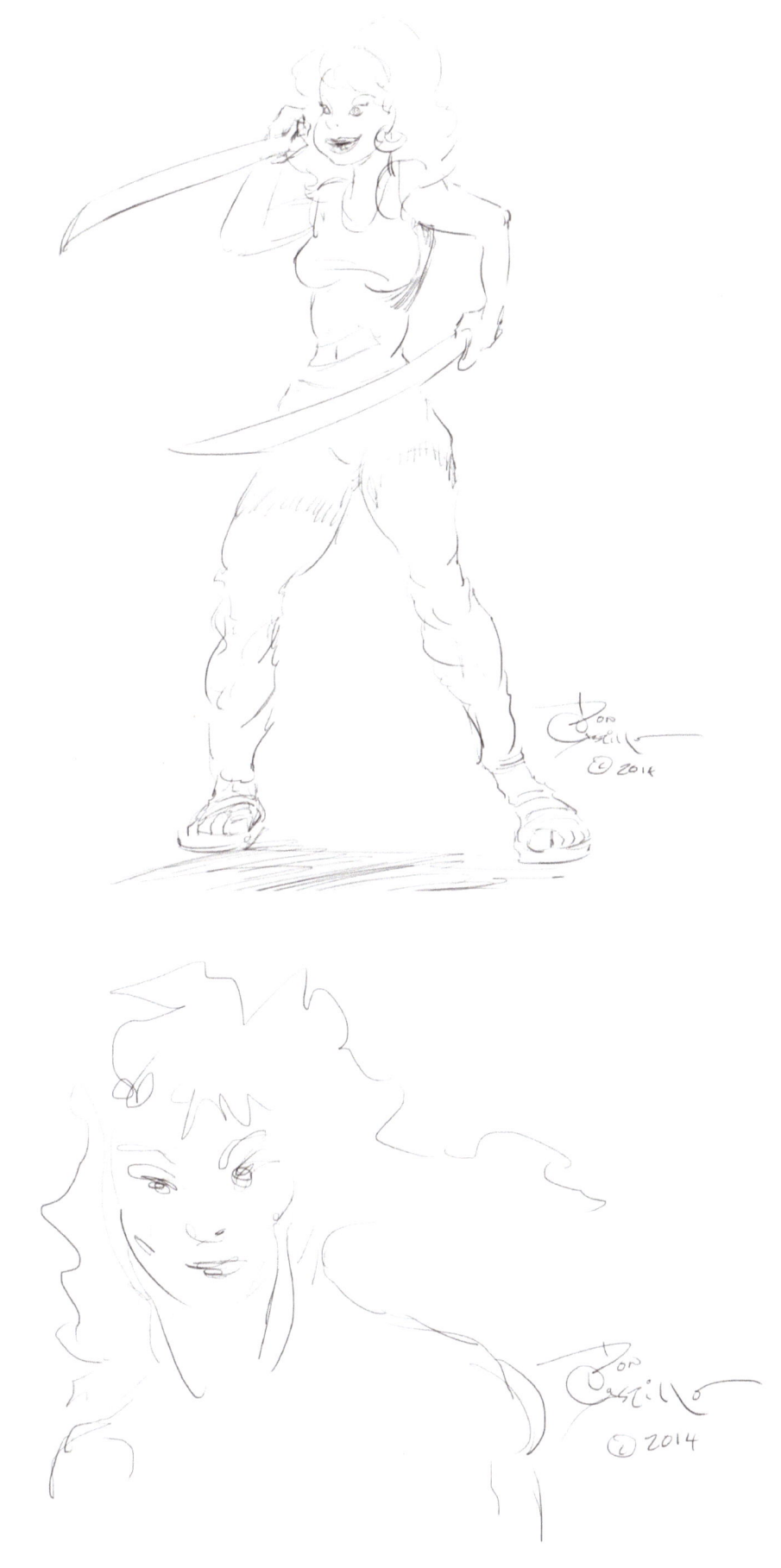

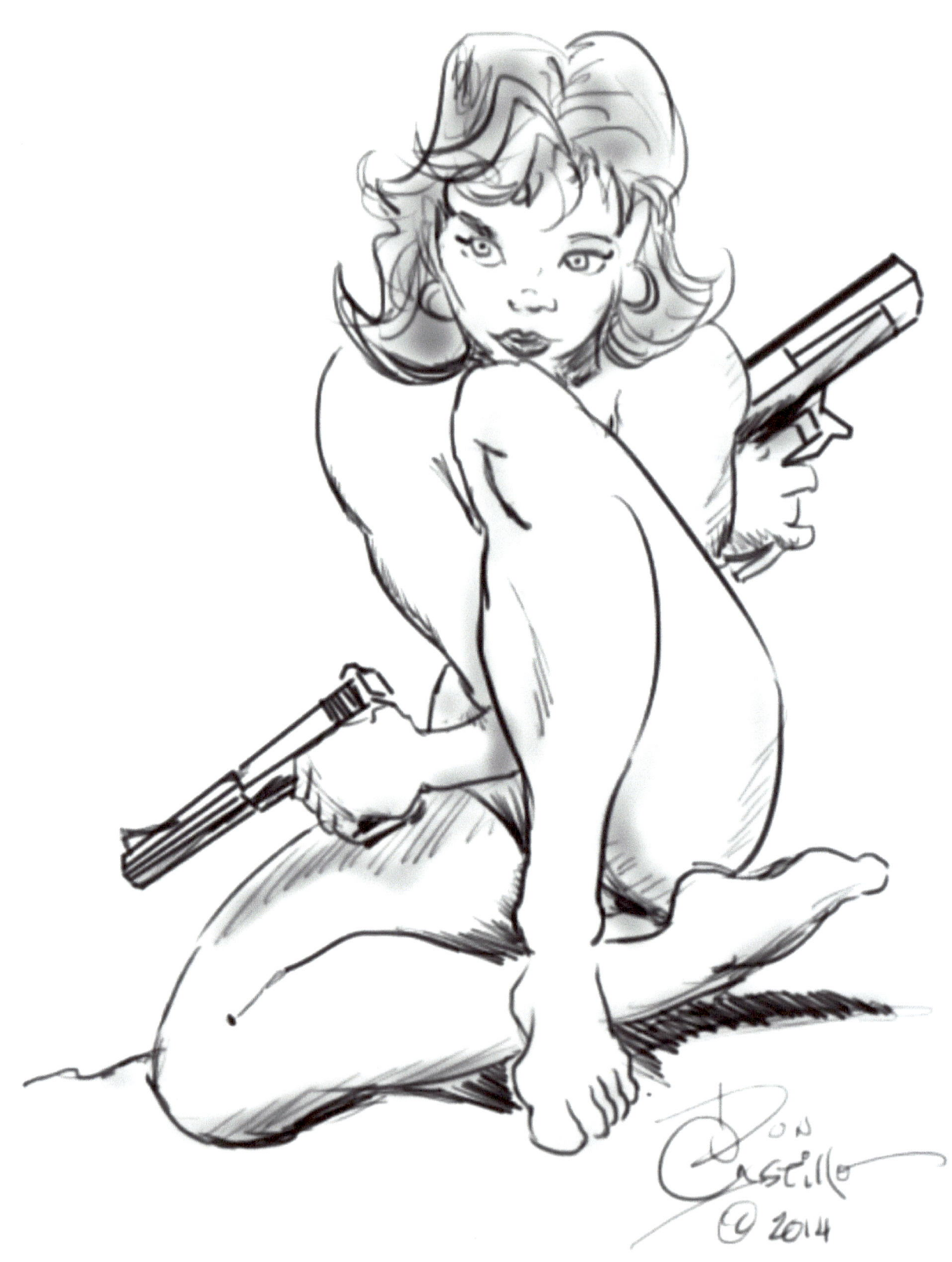

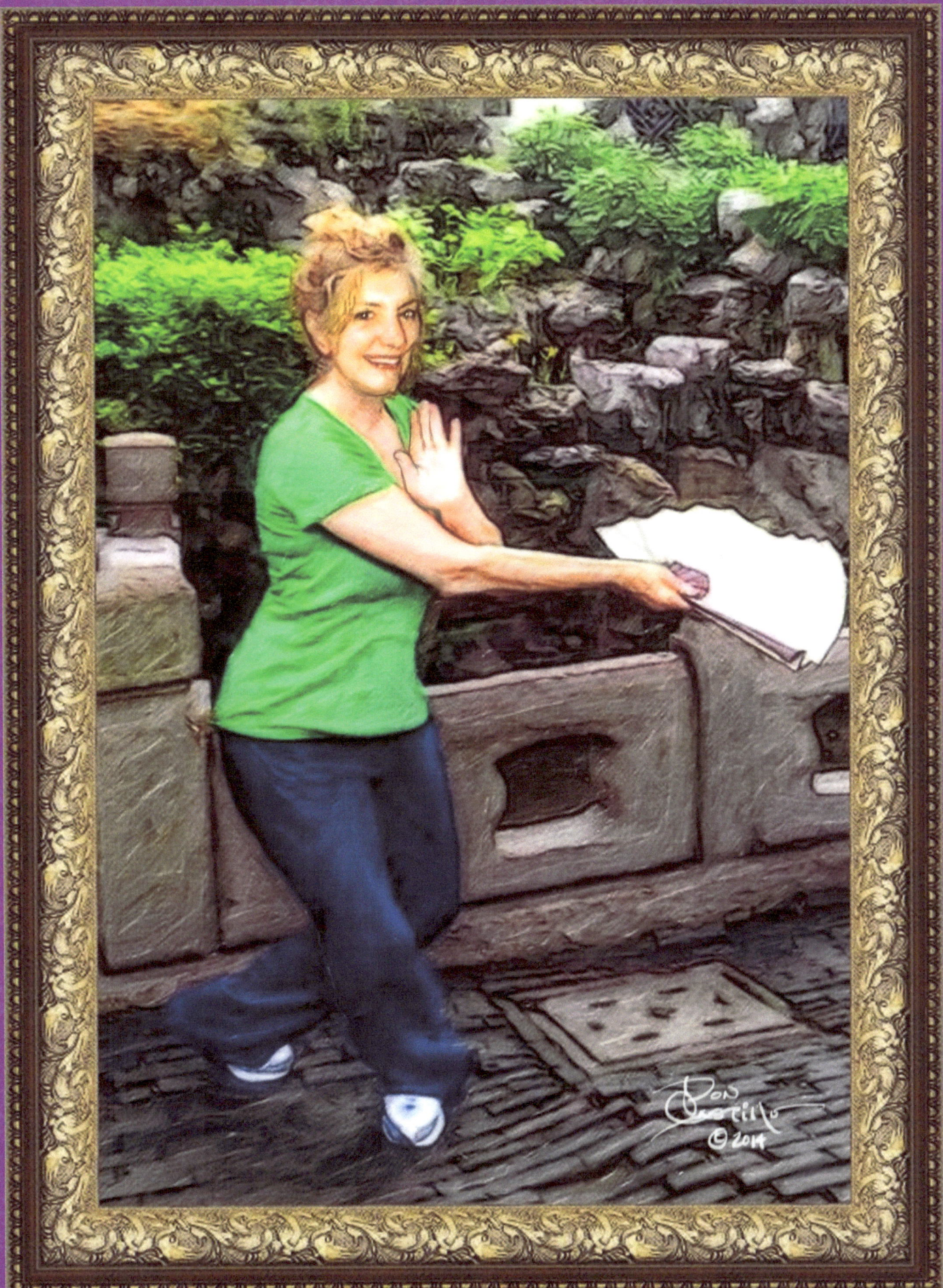

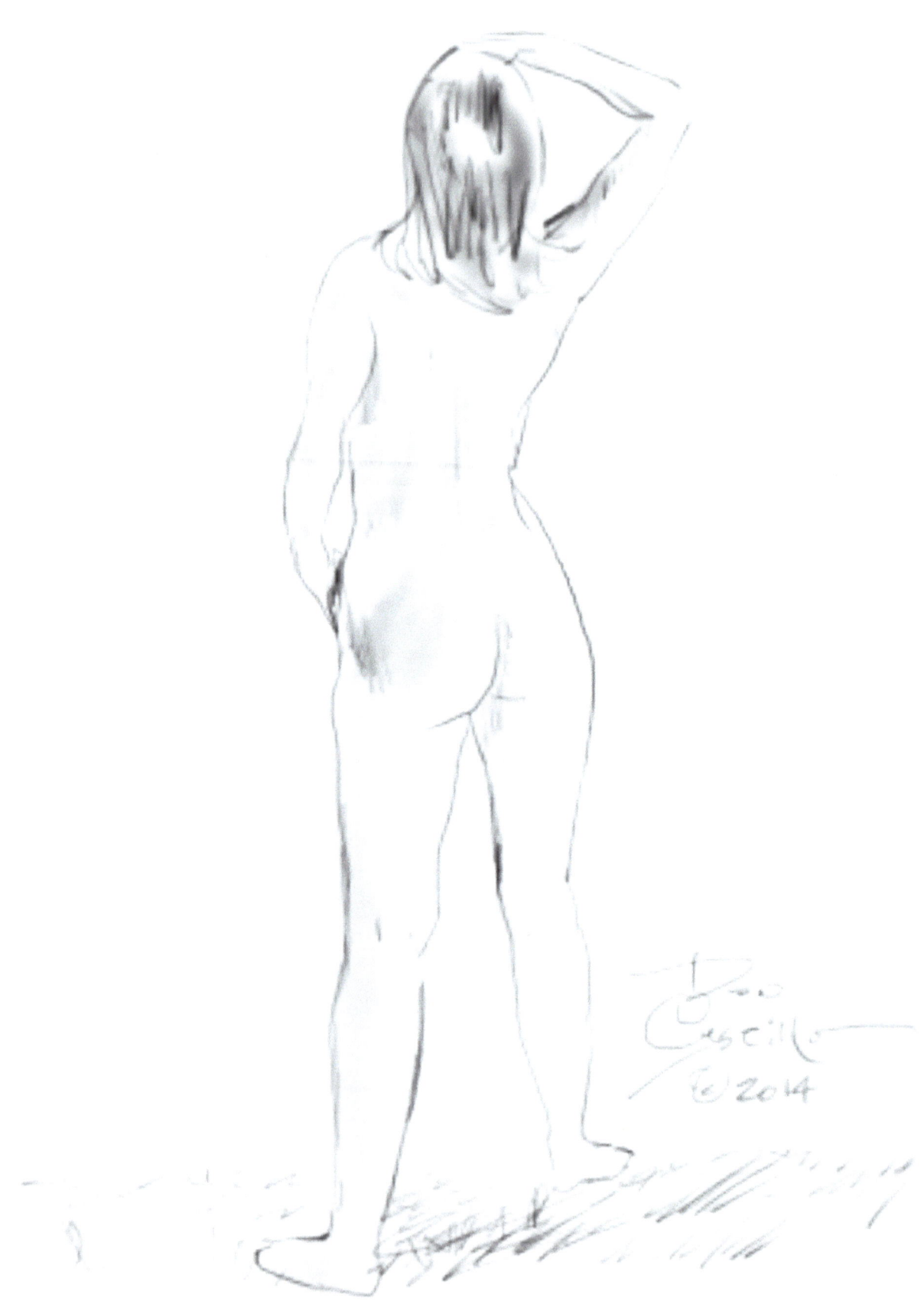

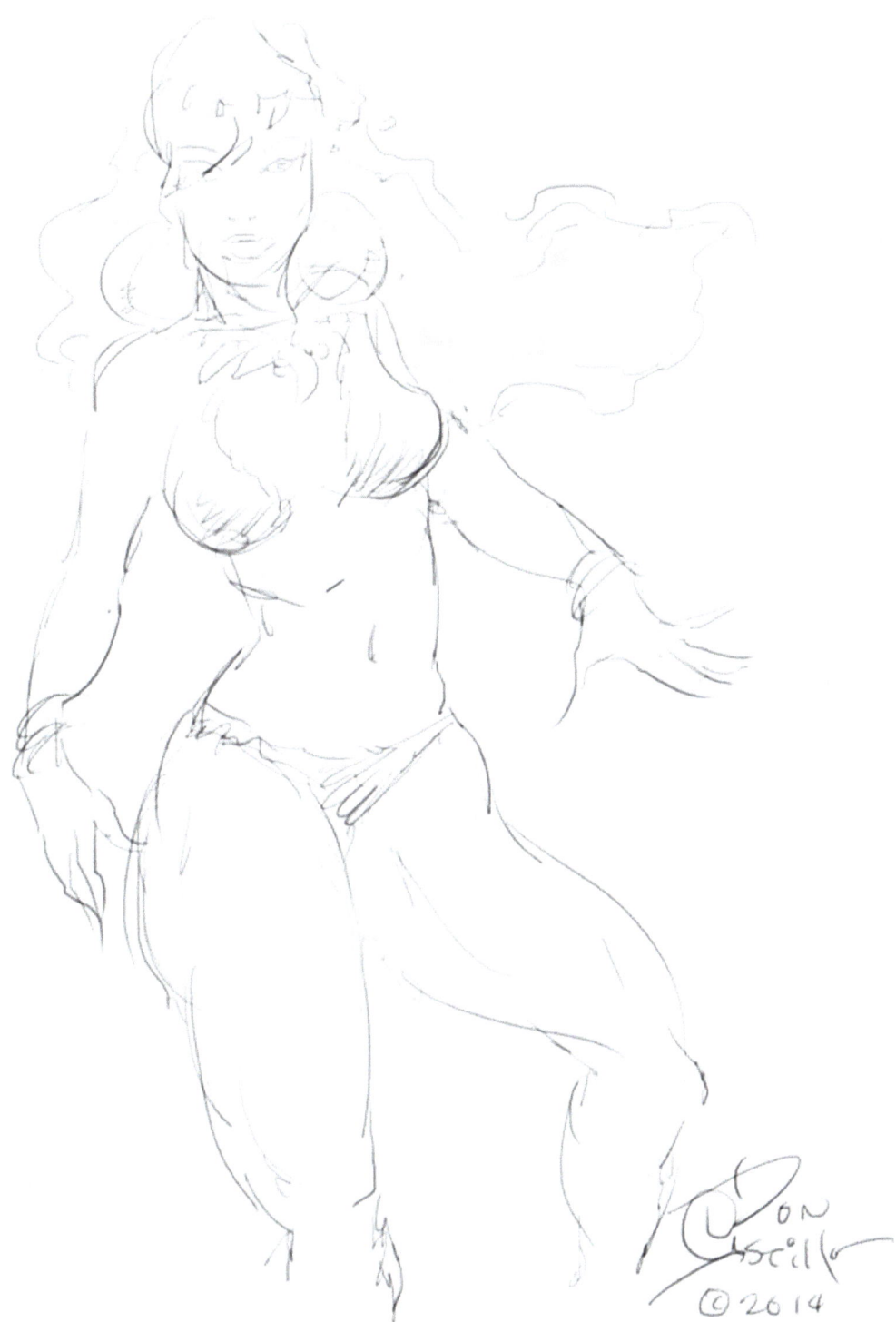

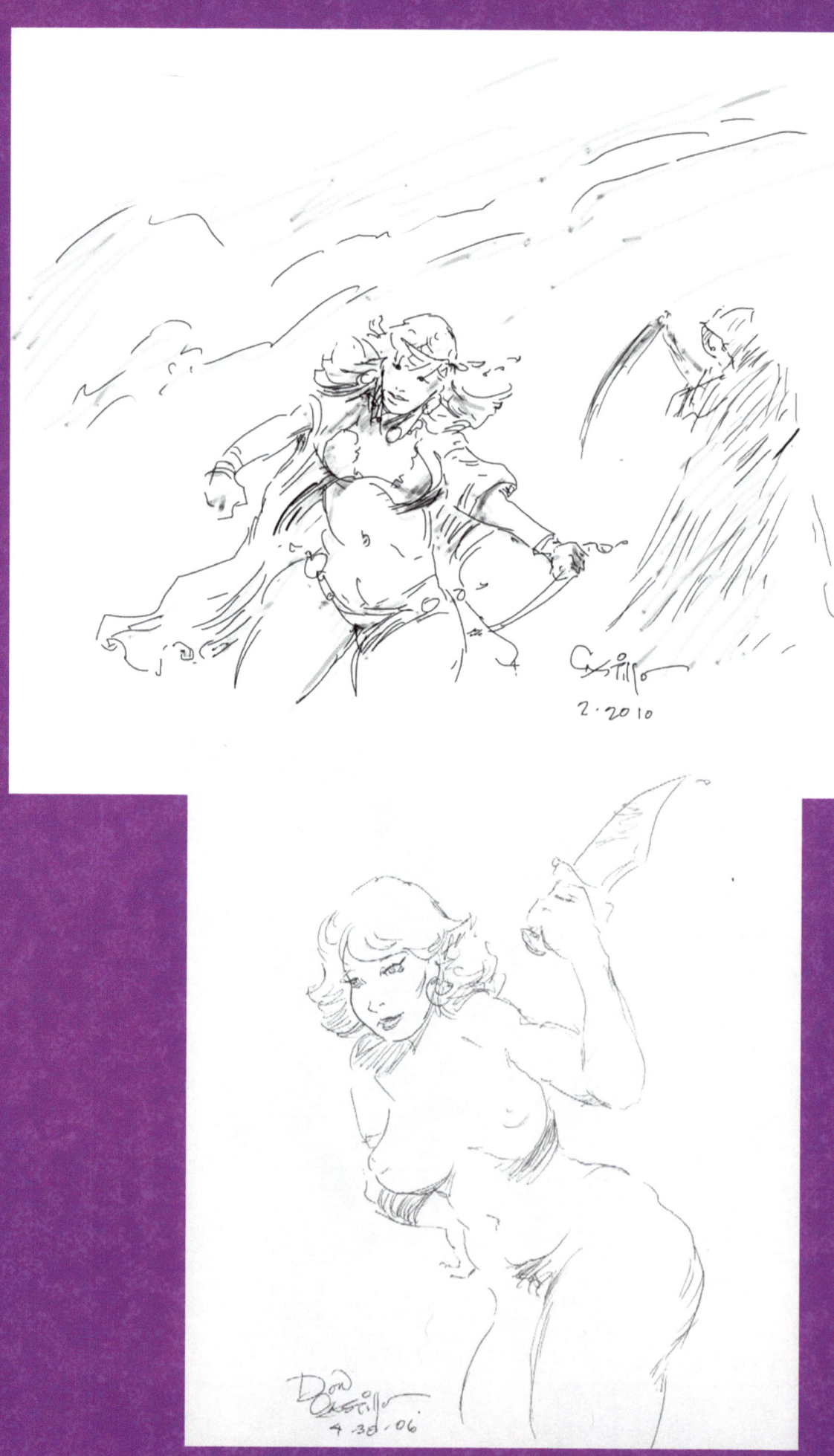

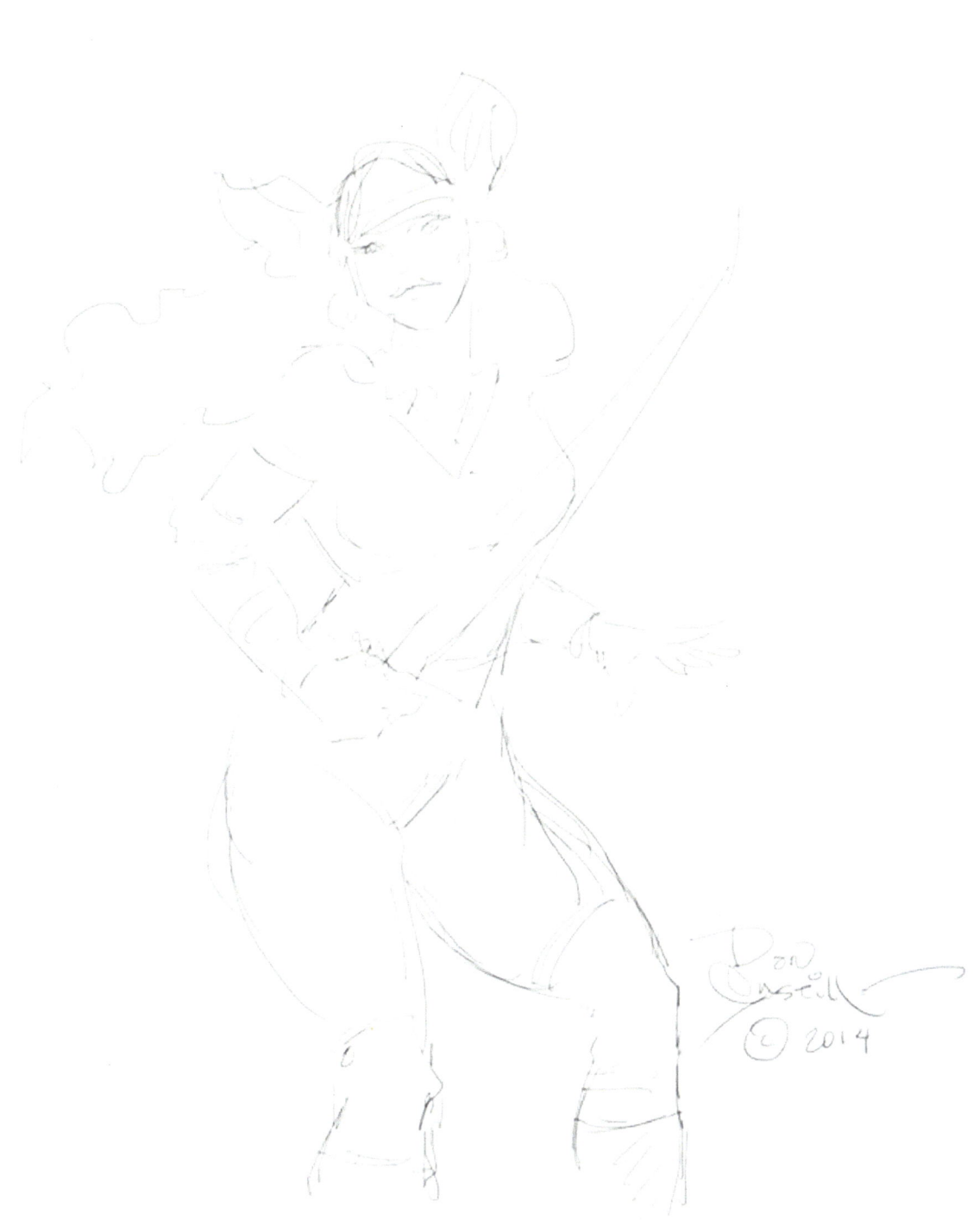

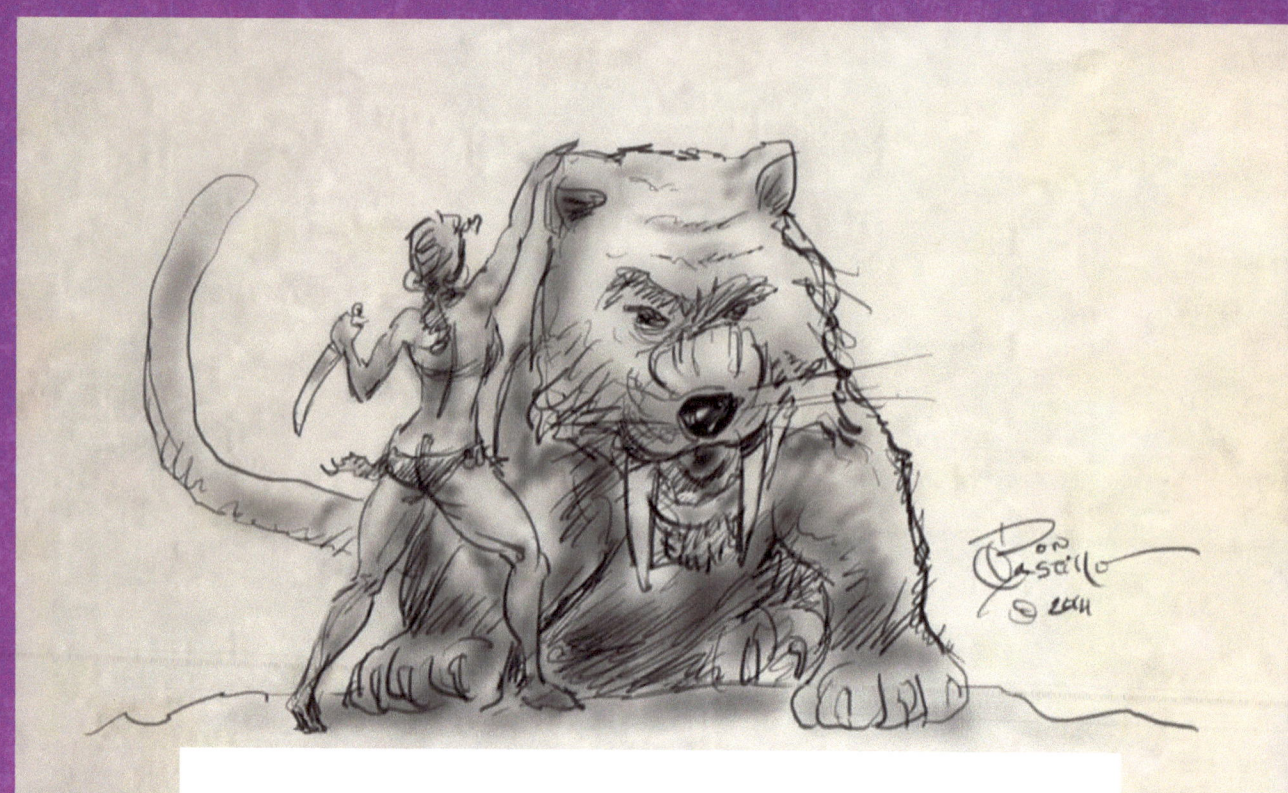

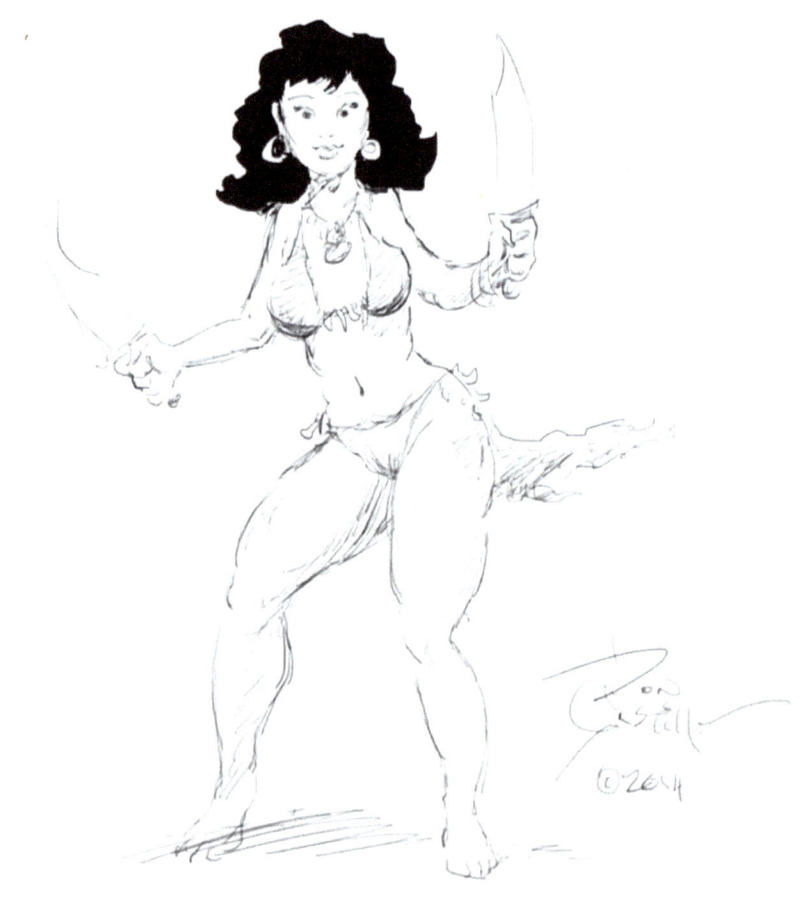

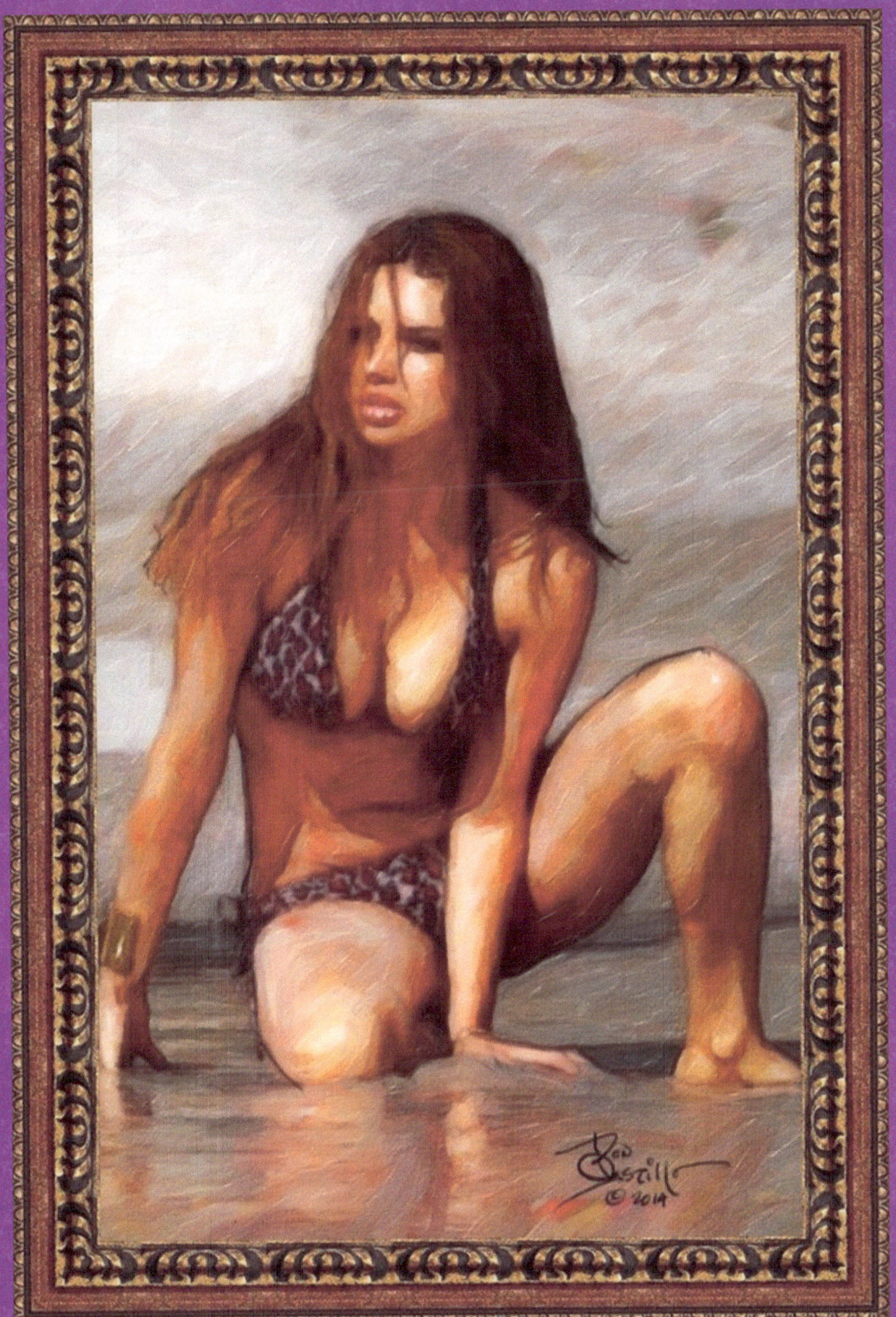

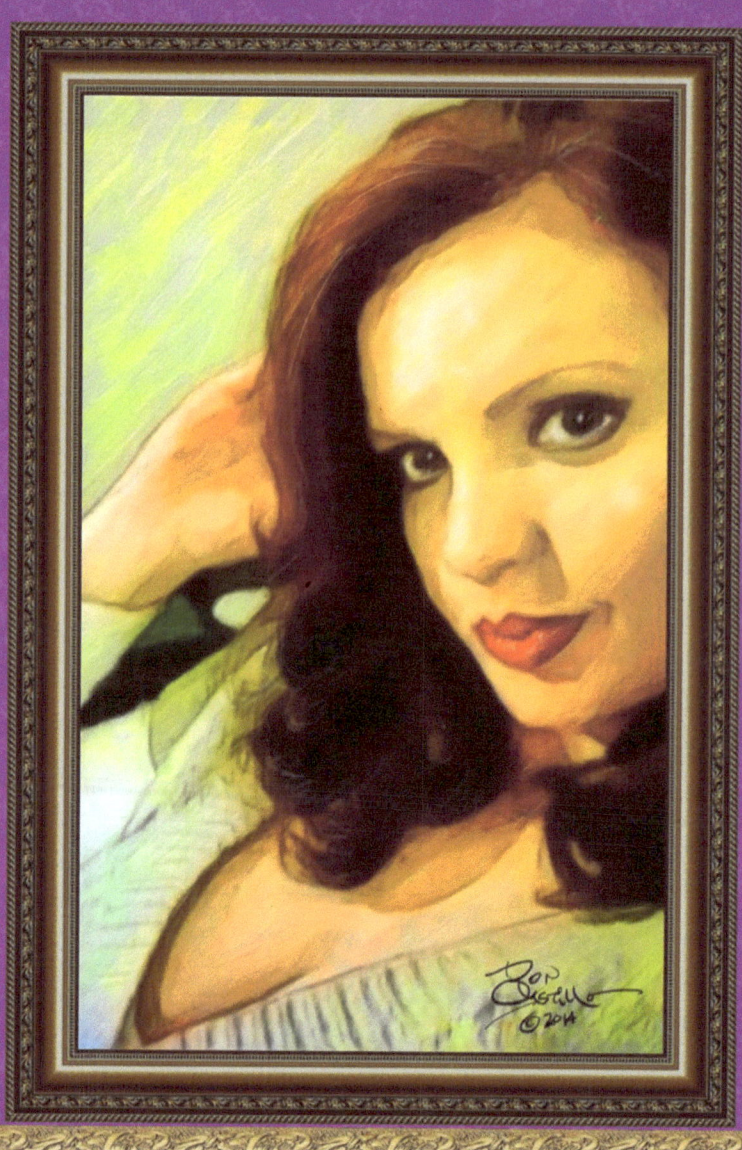

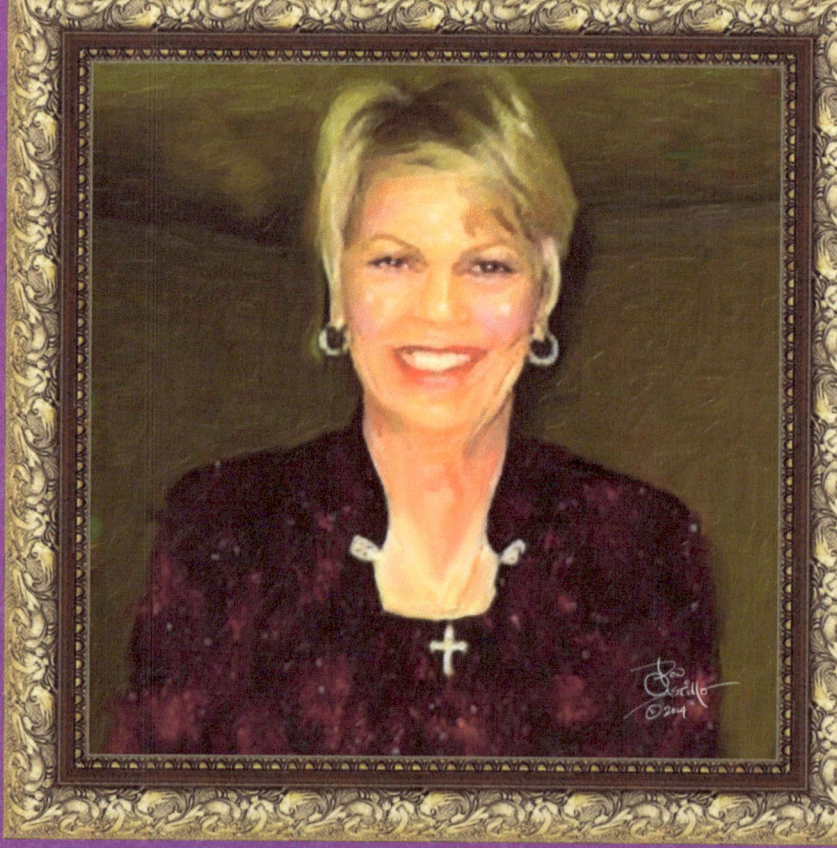

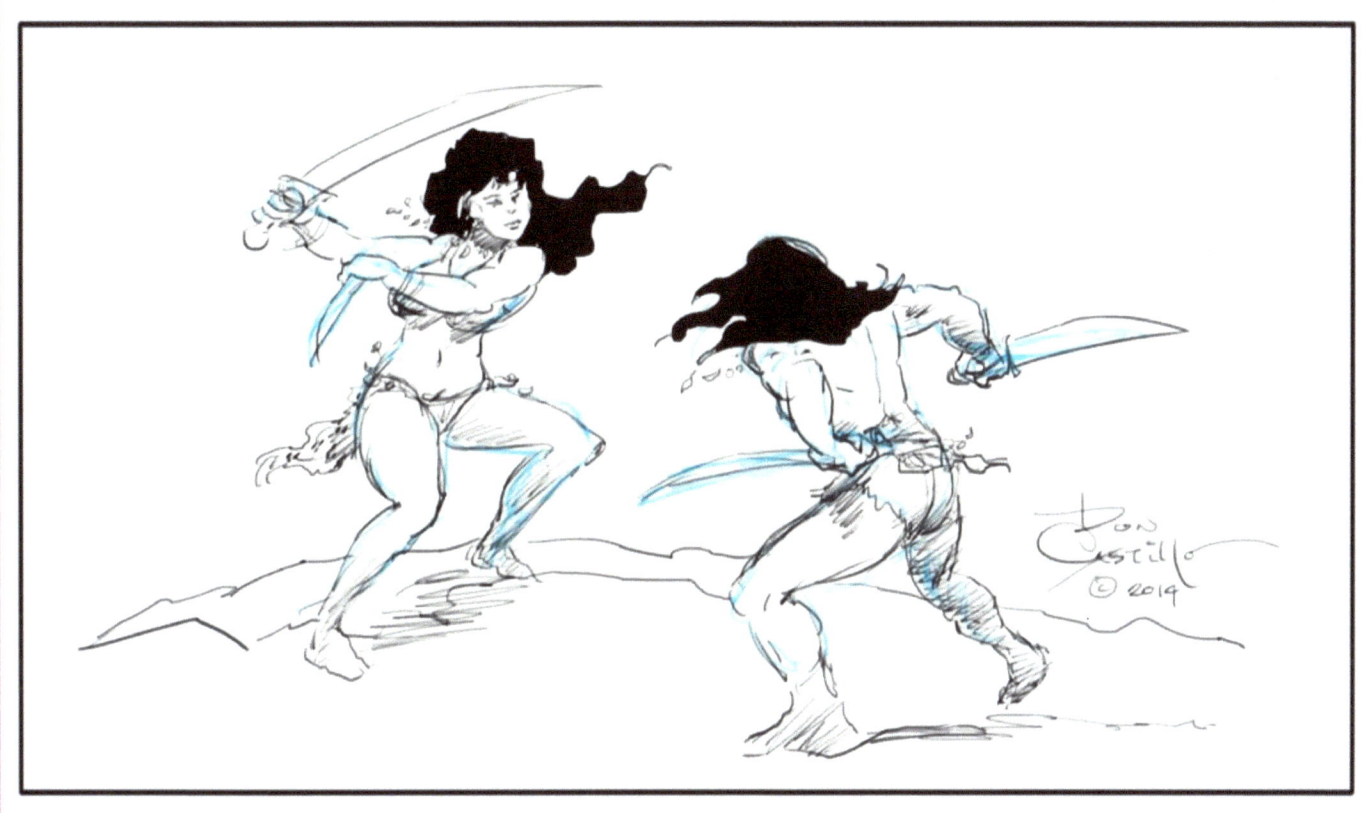

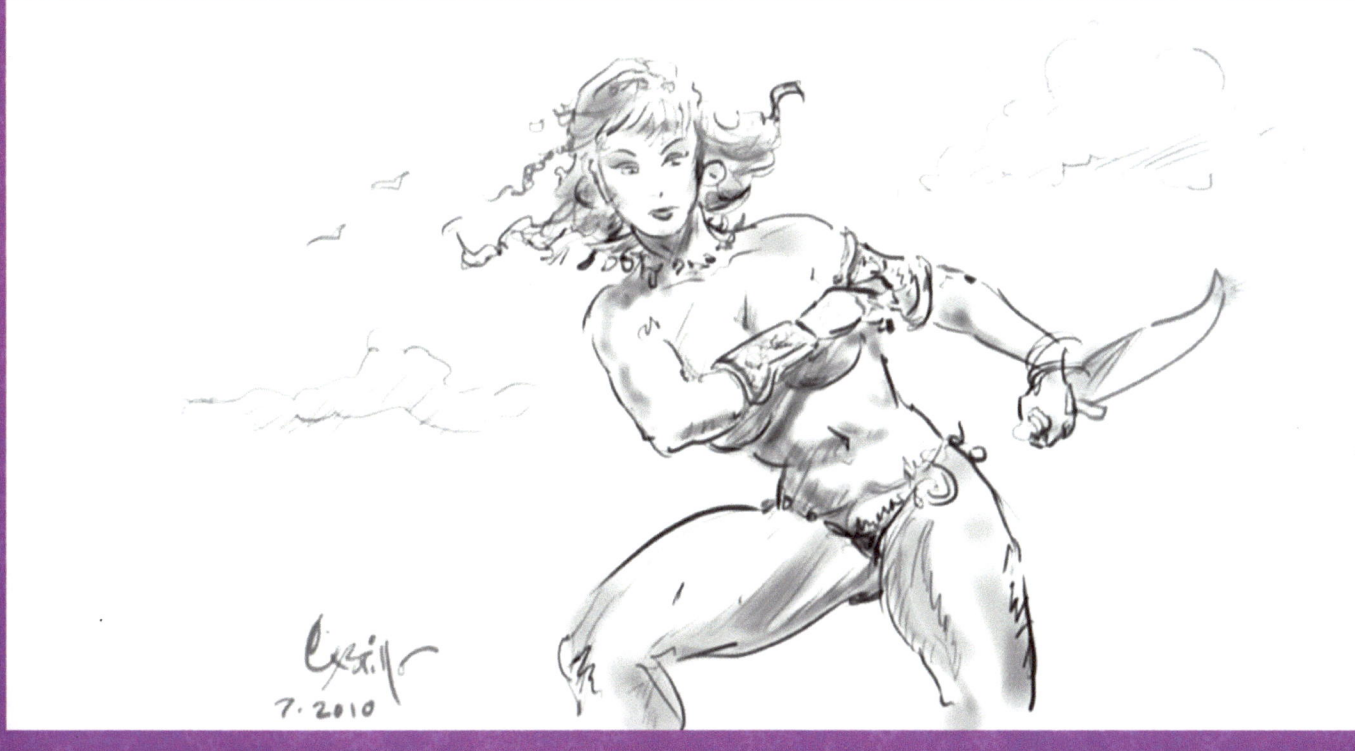

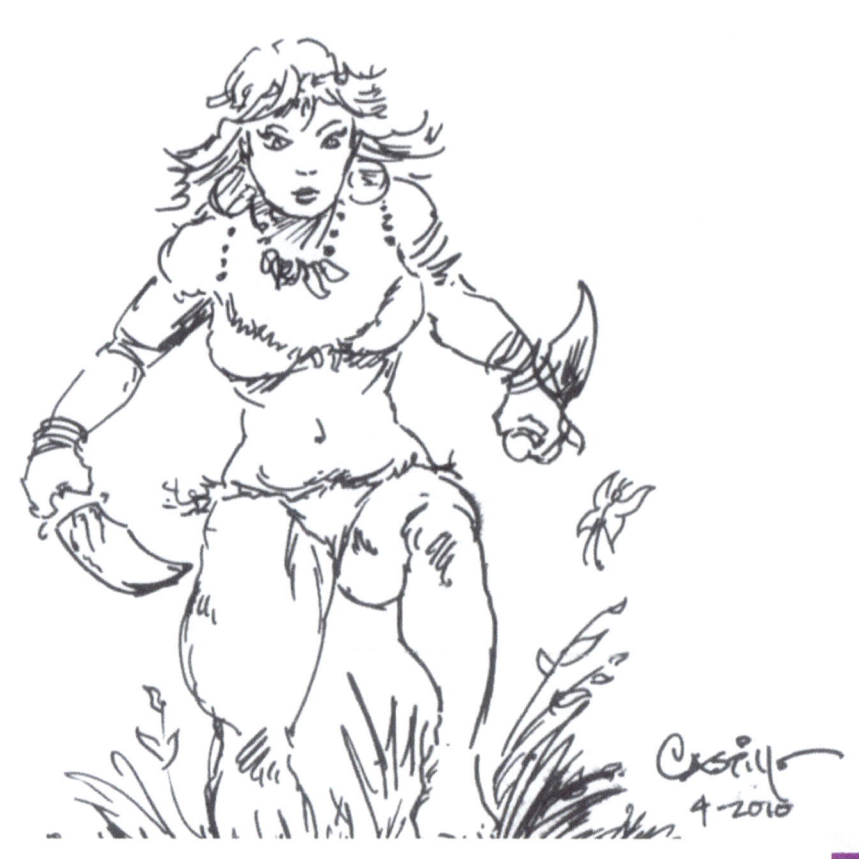

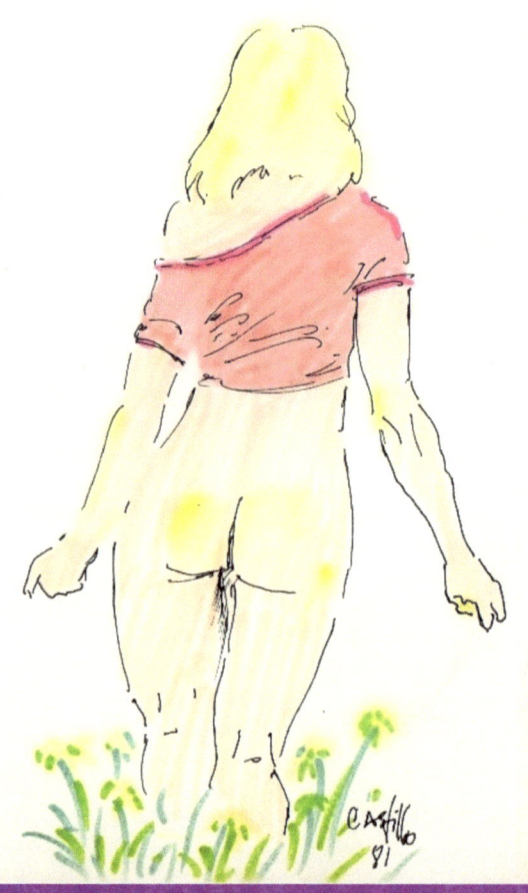

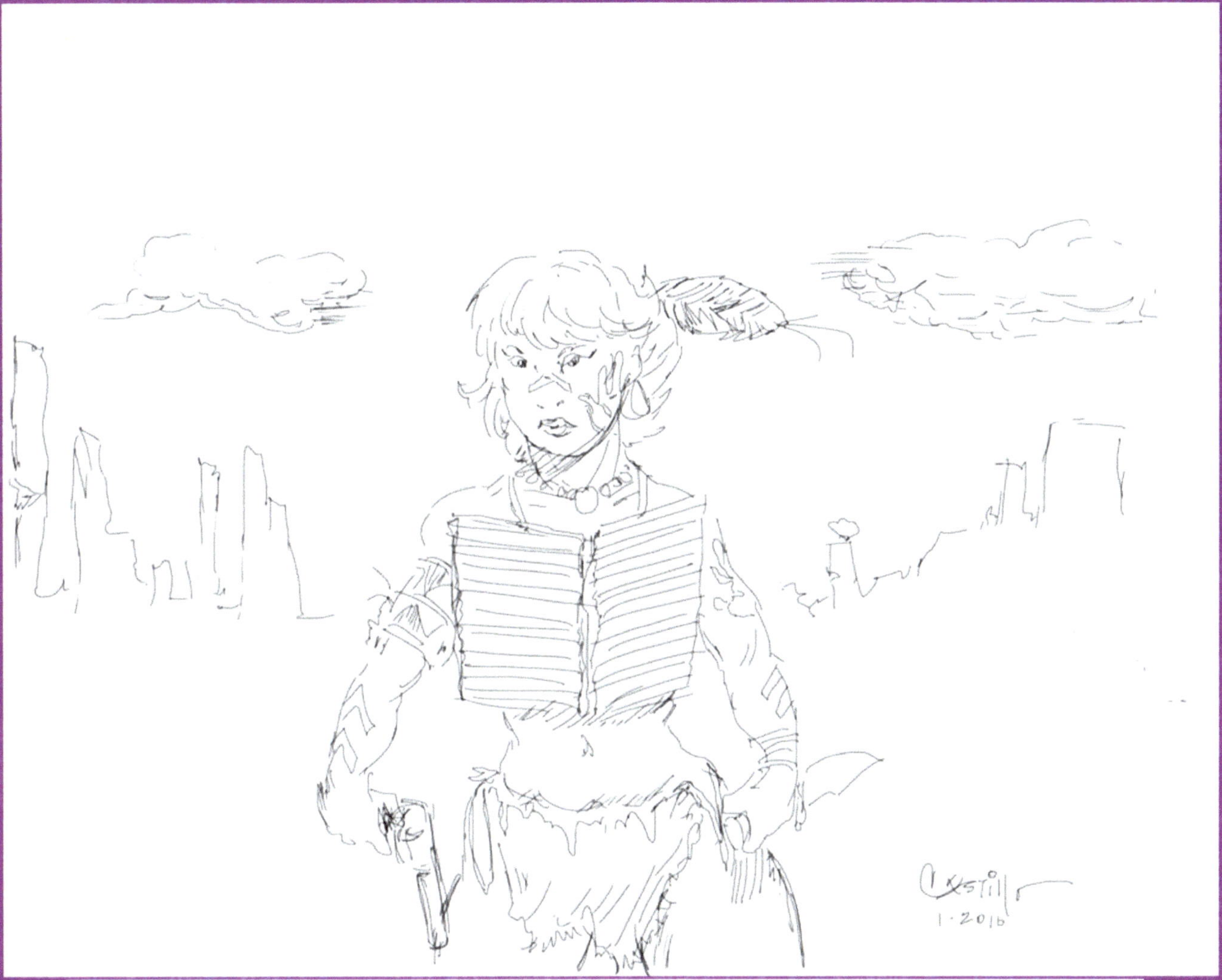

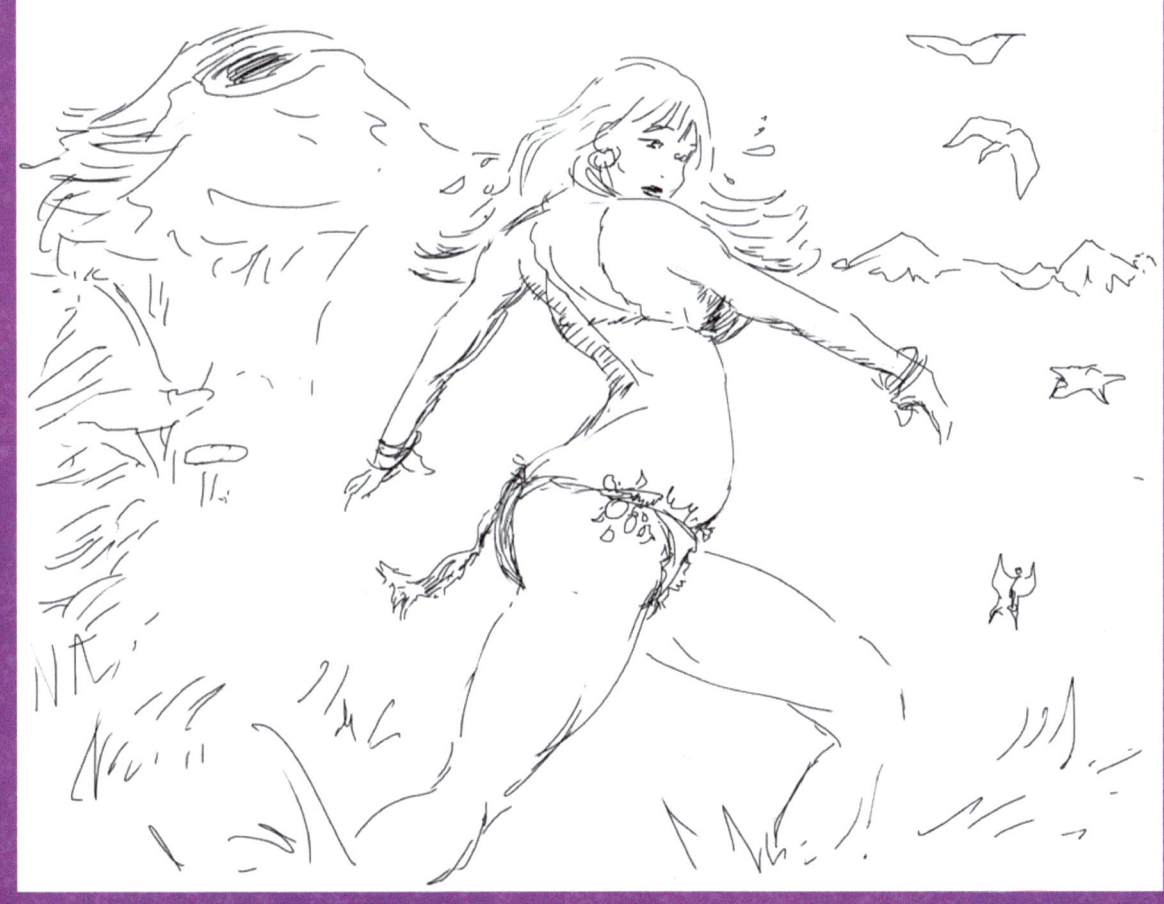

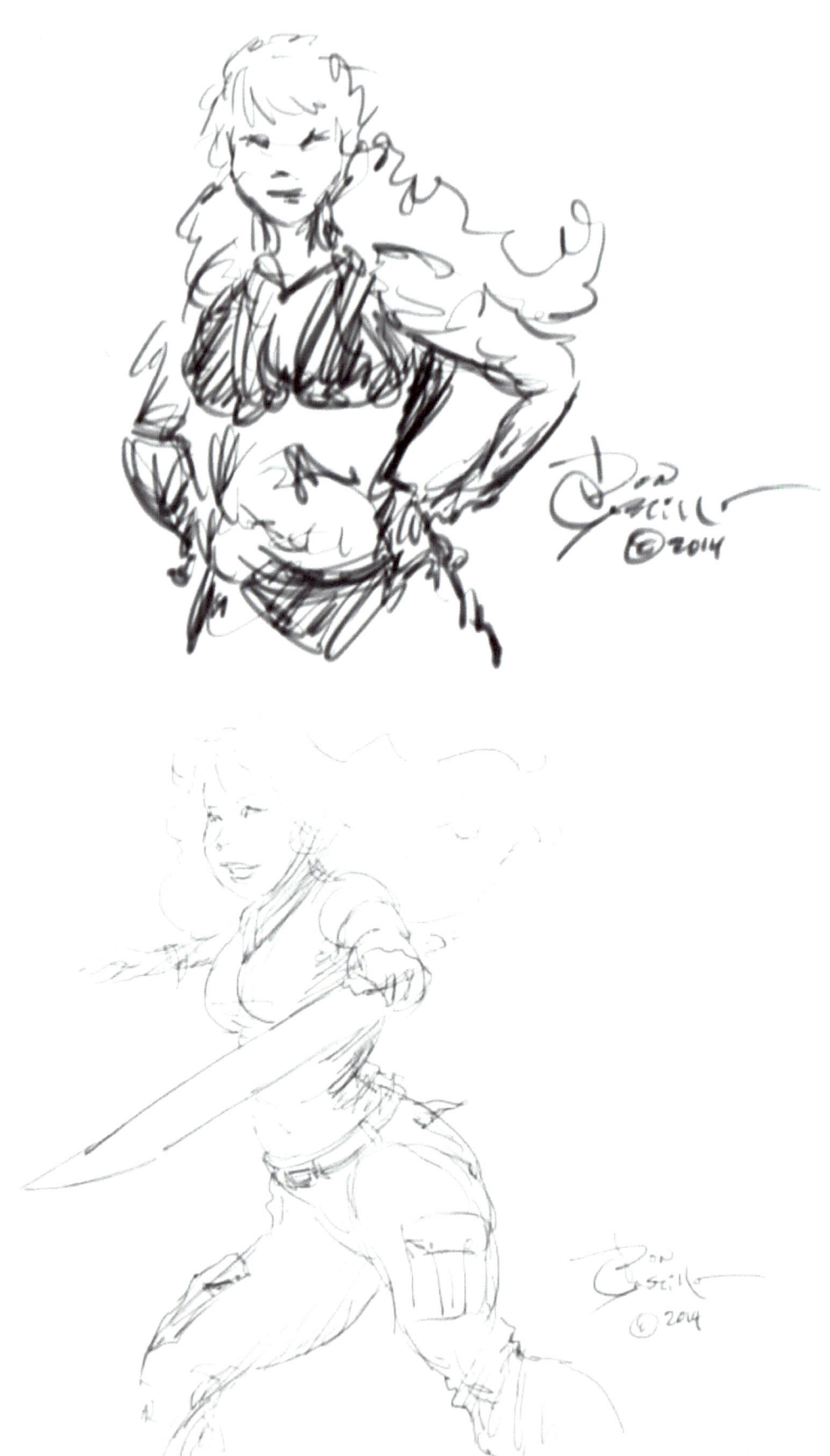

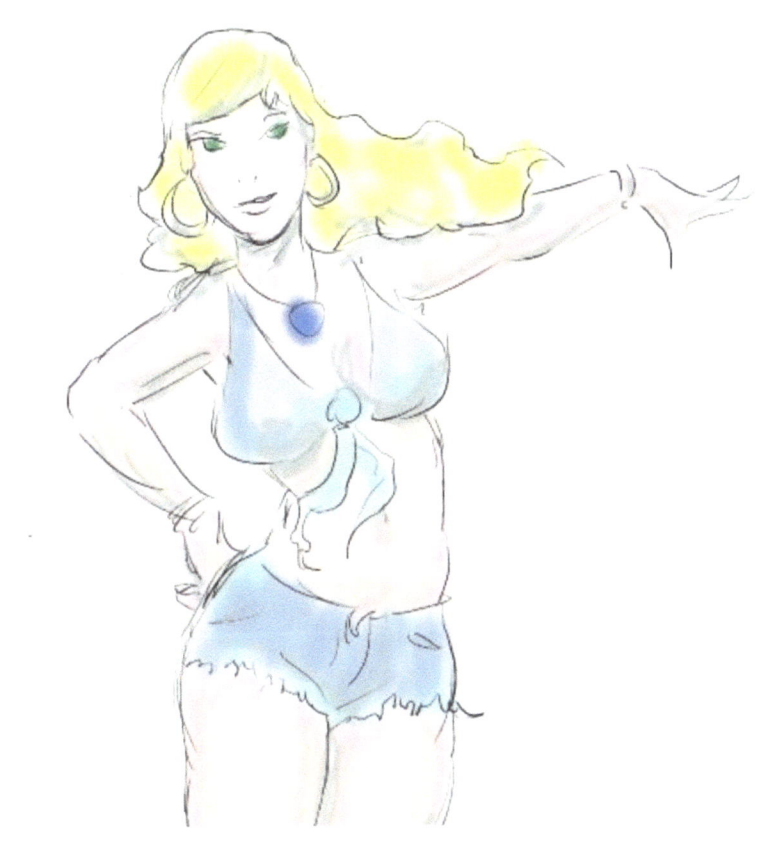

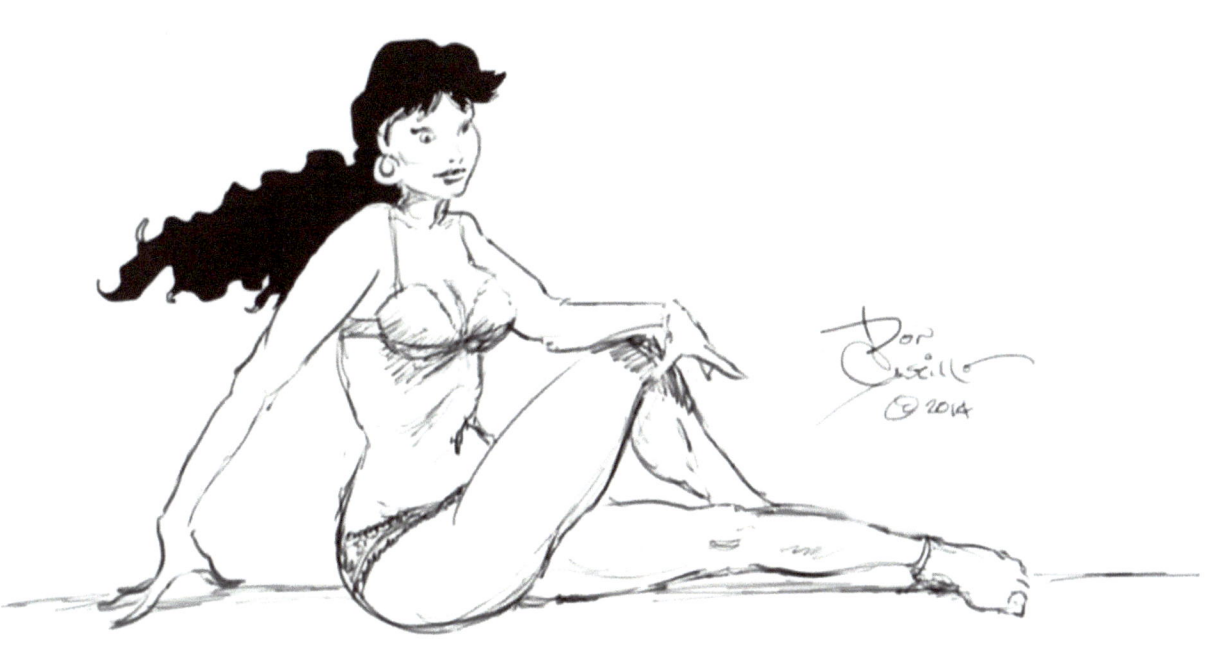

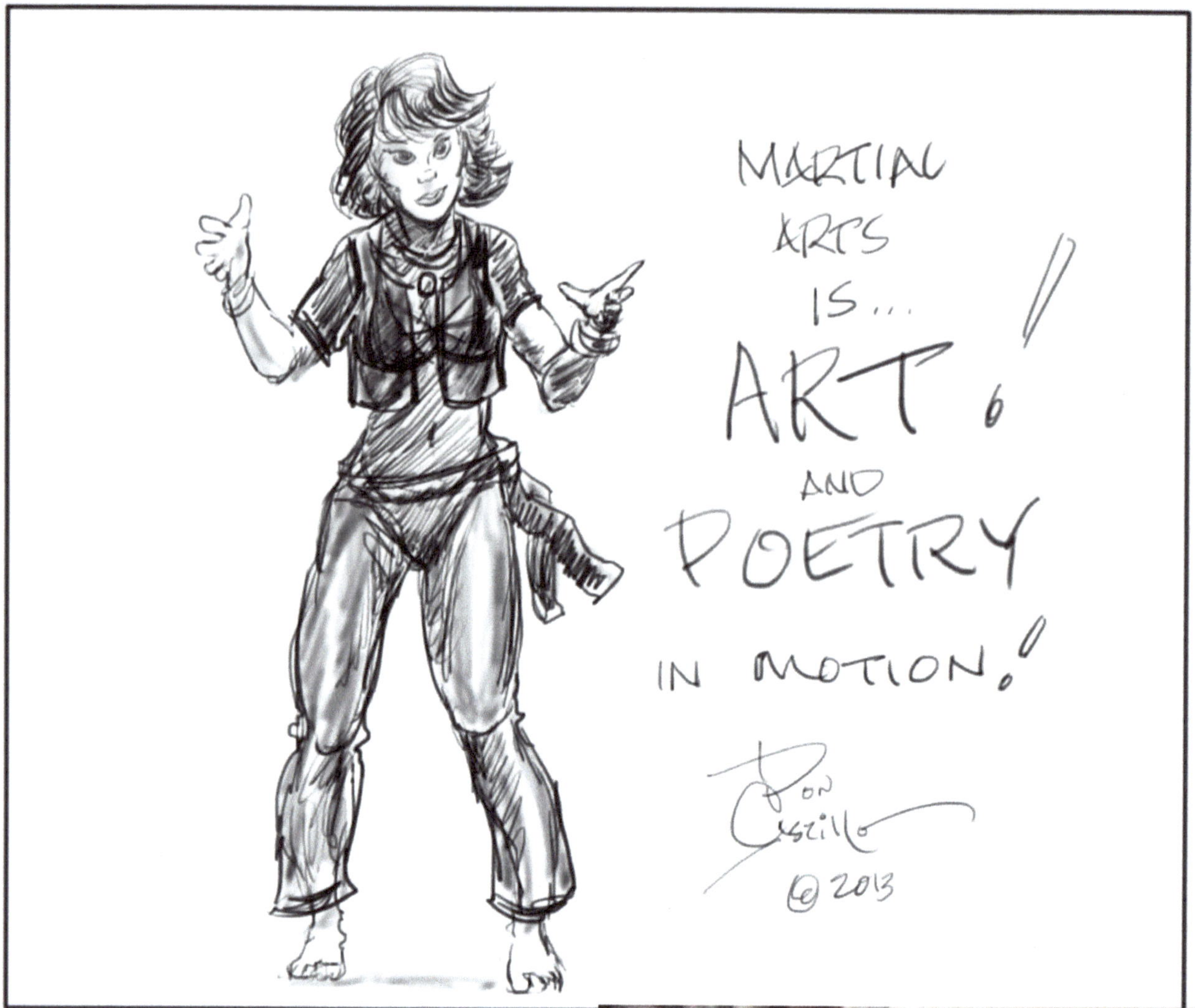

MARTIAL
ARTS
IS...
ART!
AND
POETRY
IN MOTION!

Don Castillo
© 2013

Zoei

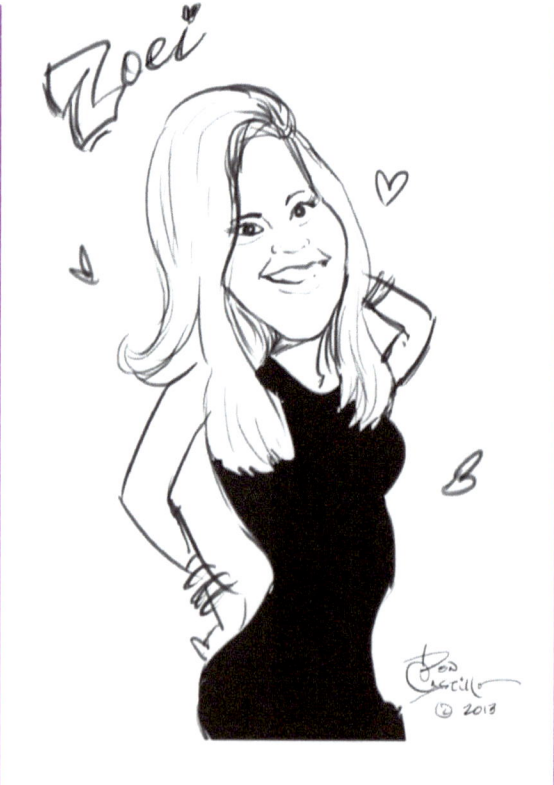

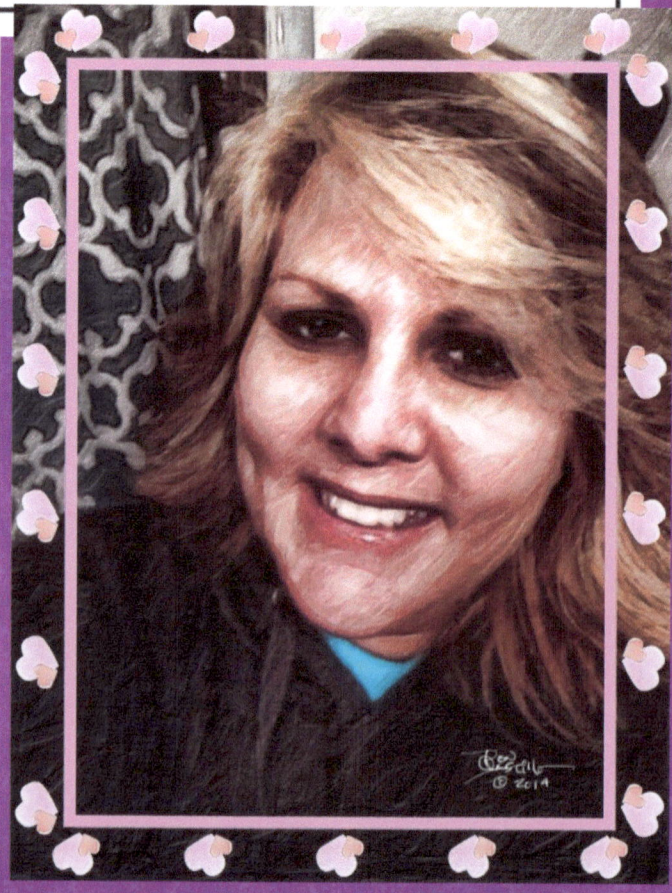

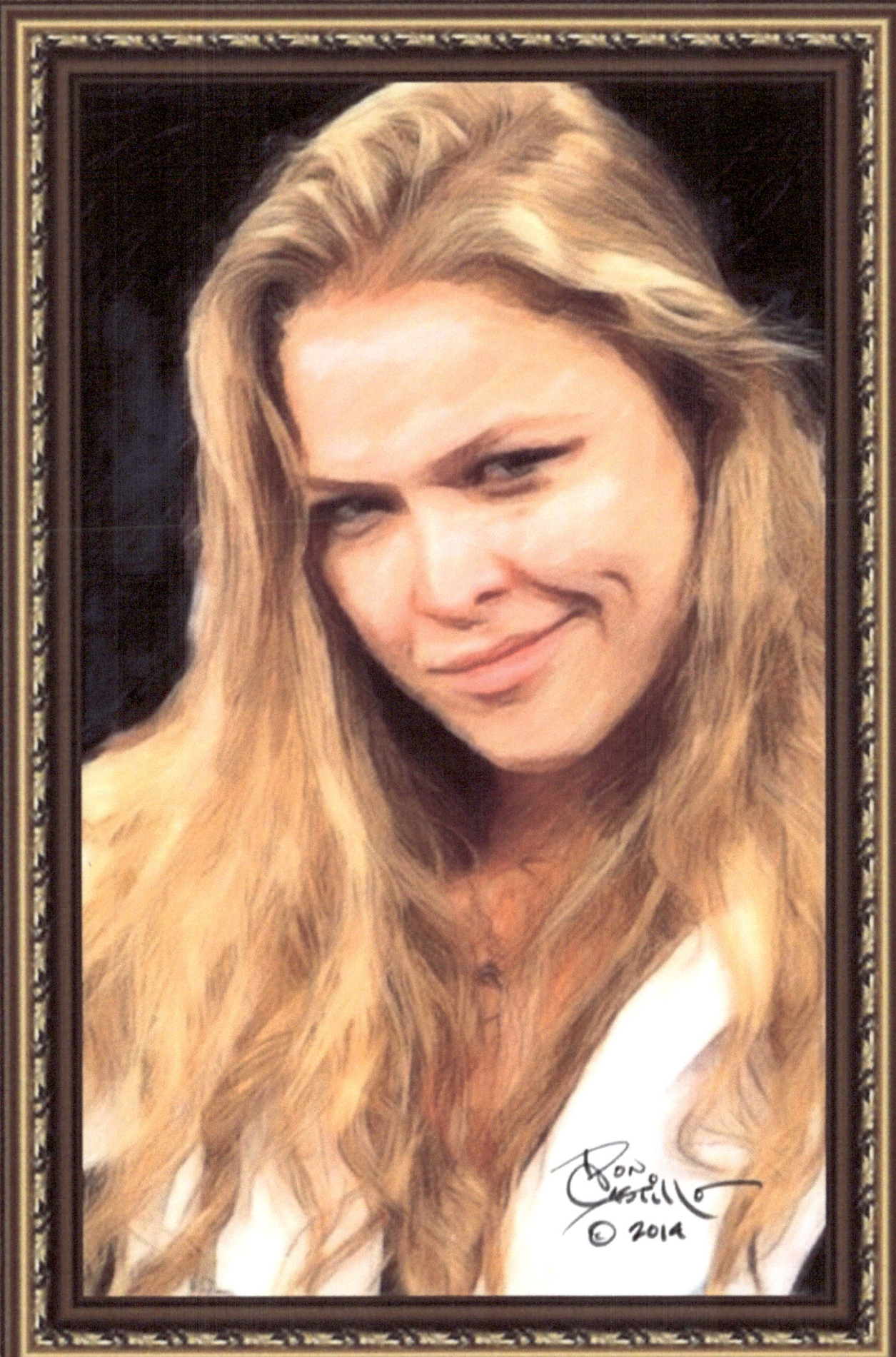

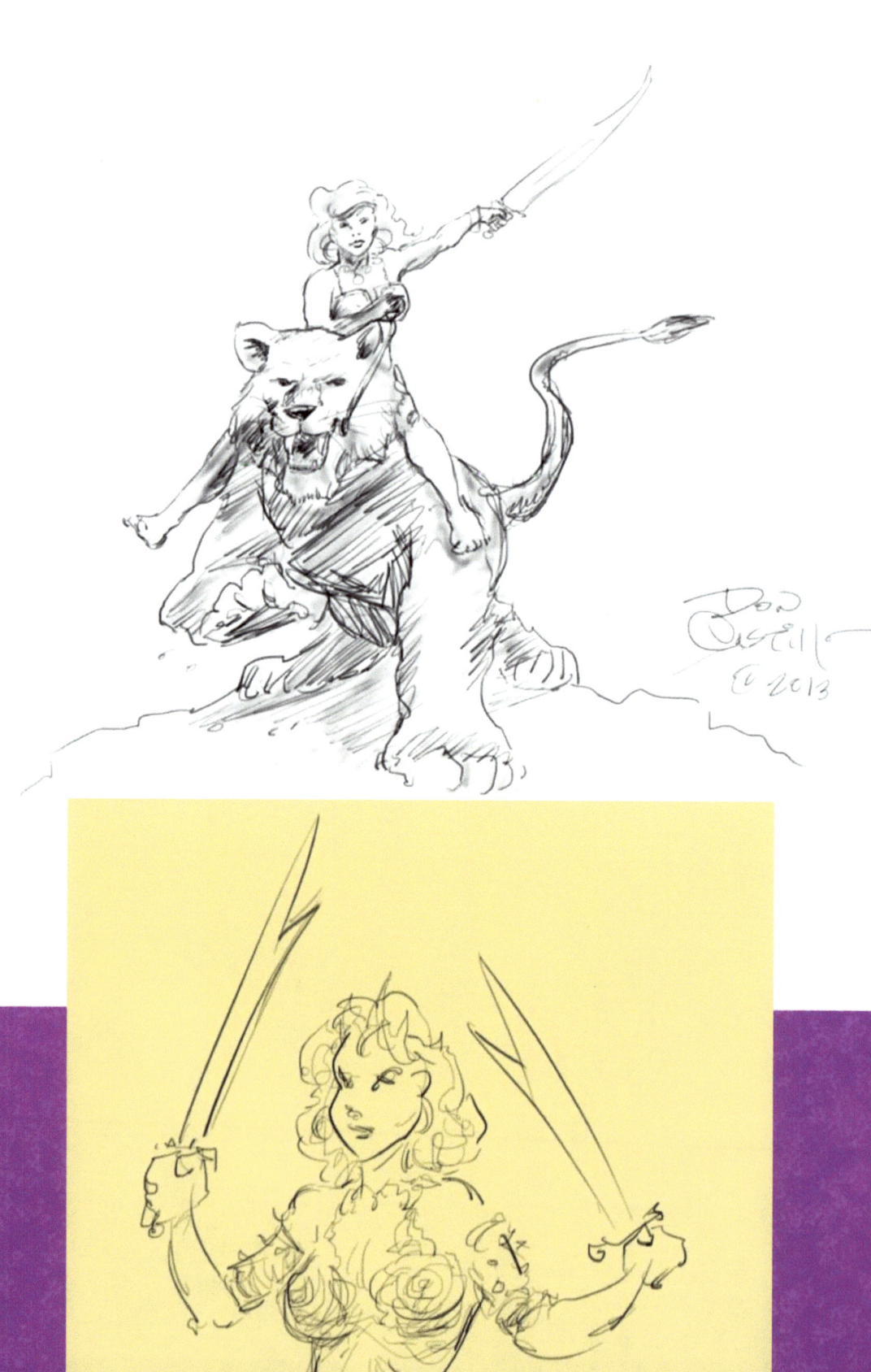

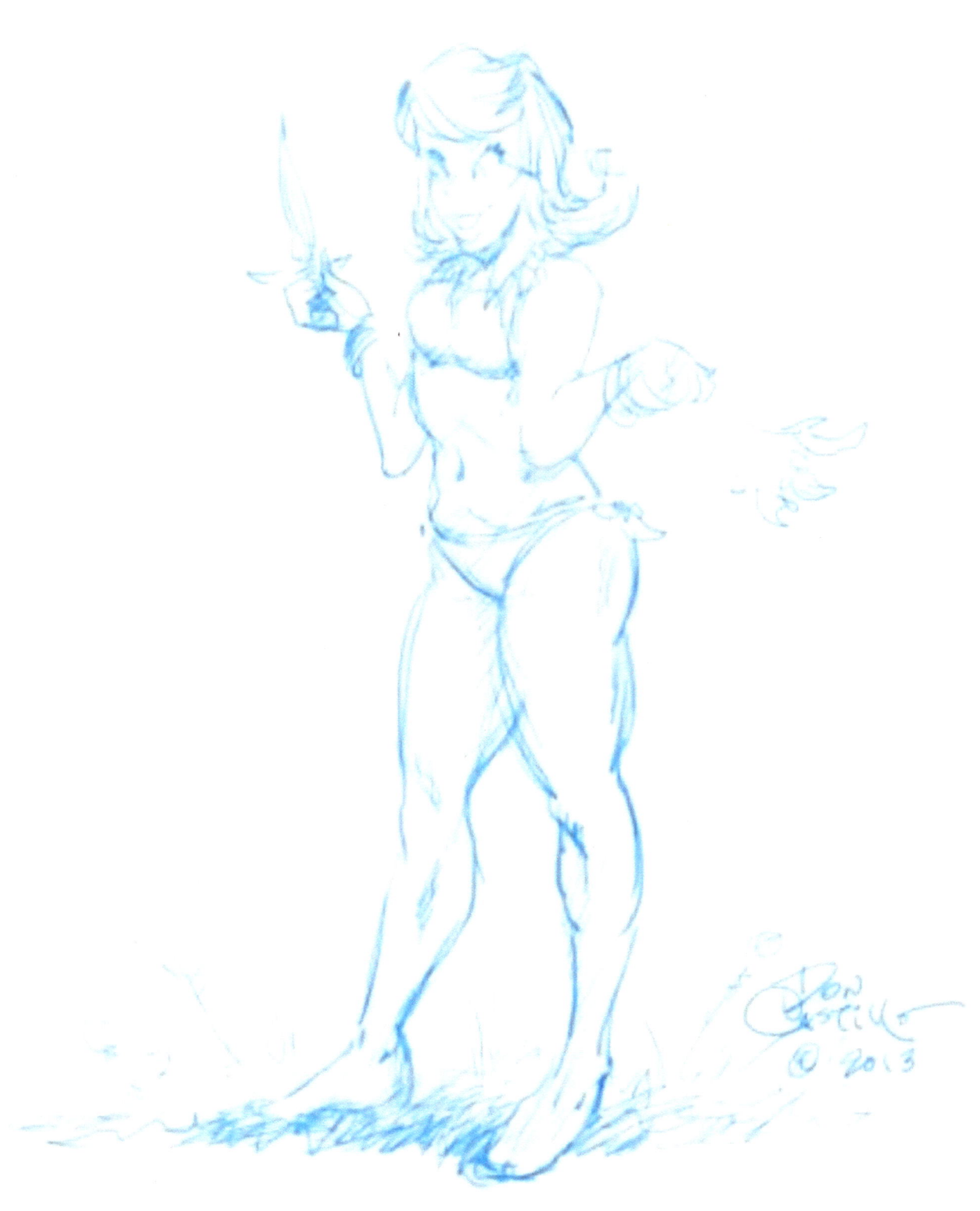

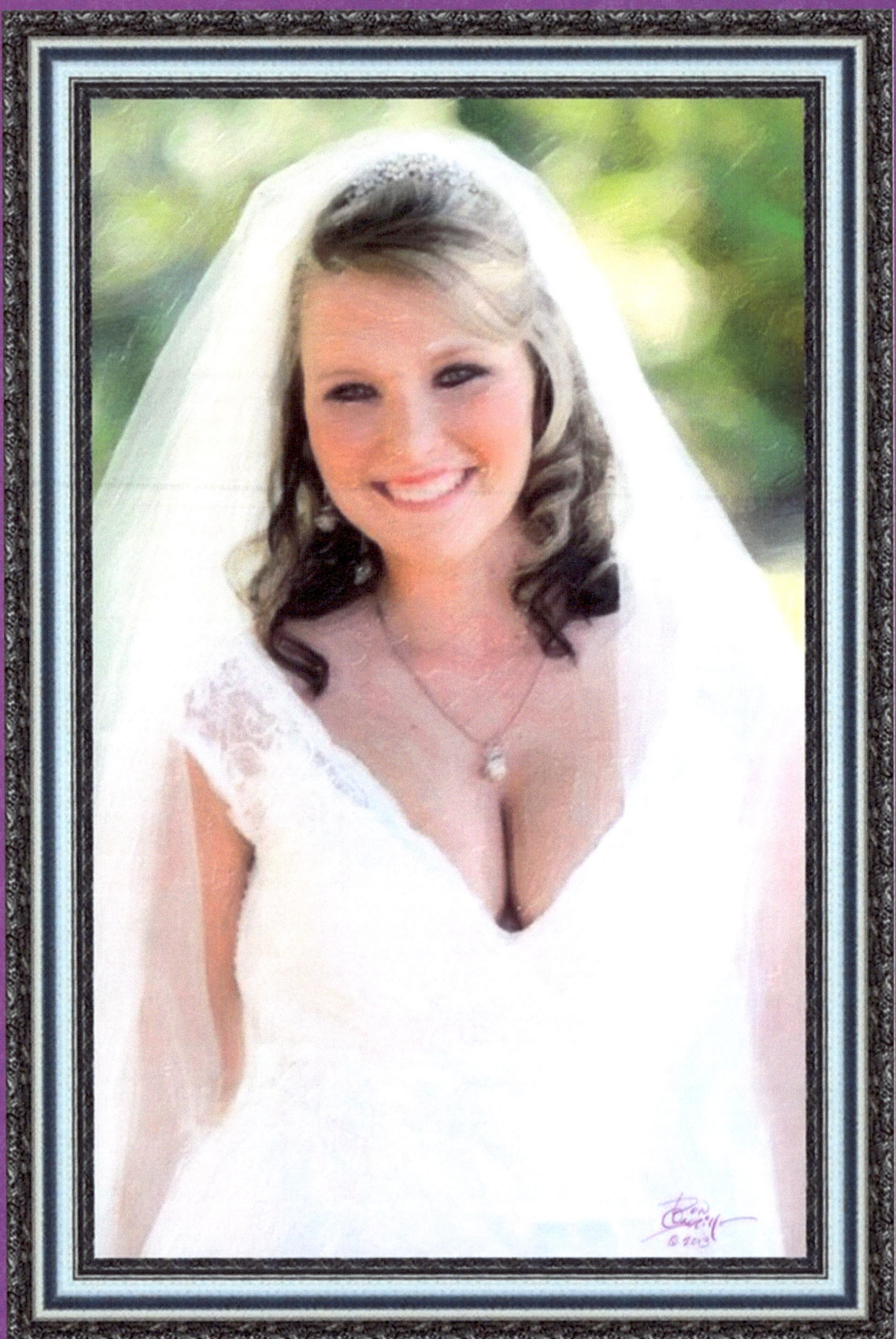

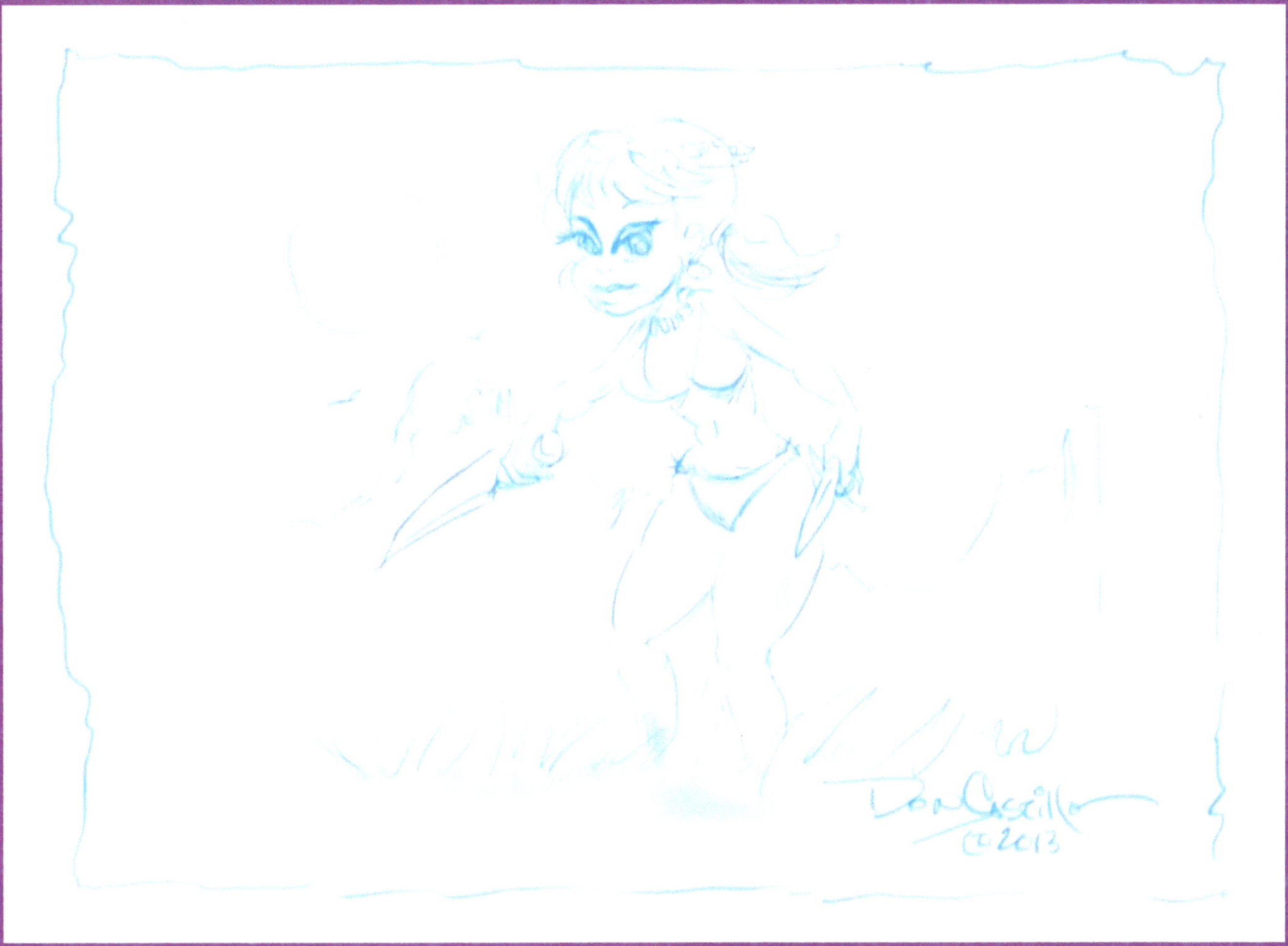

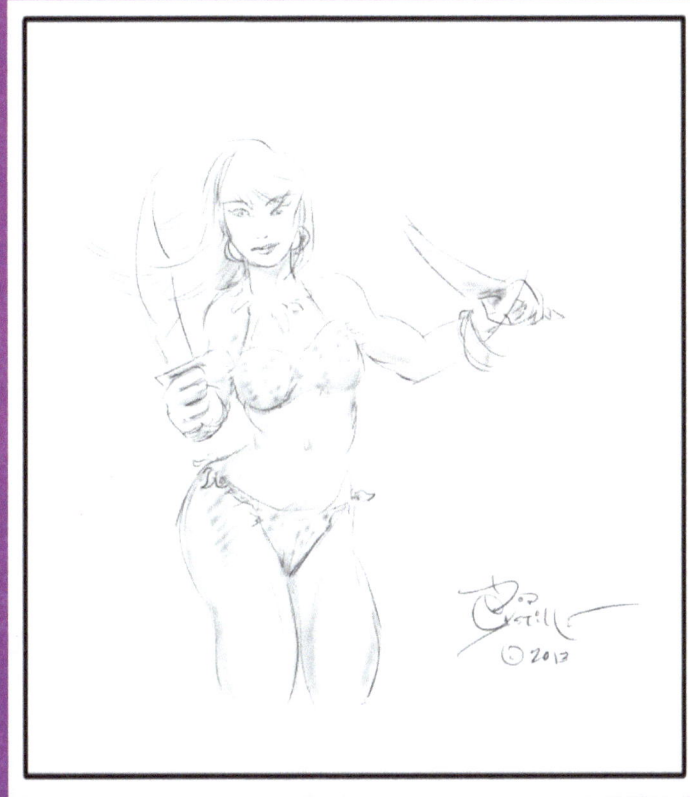

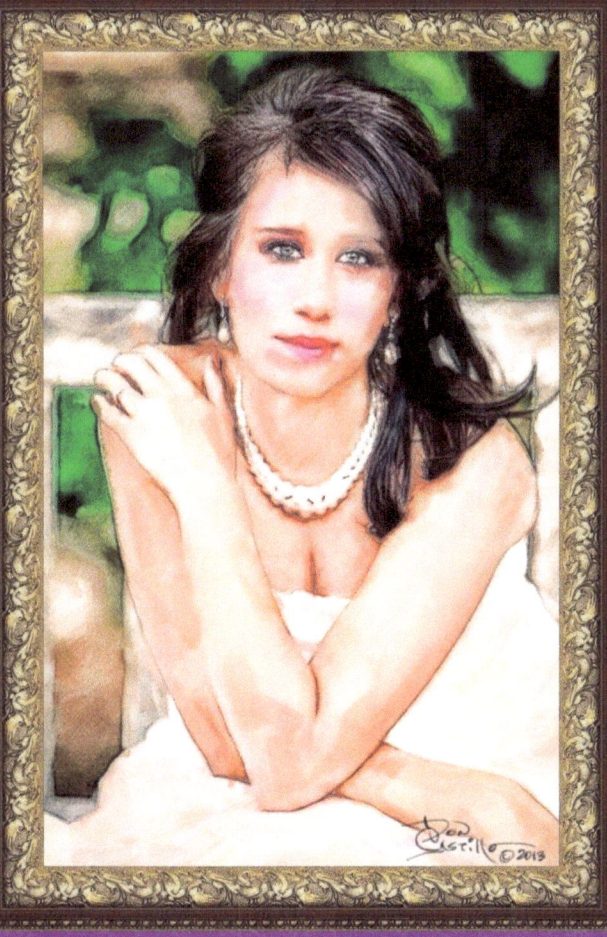

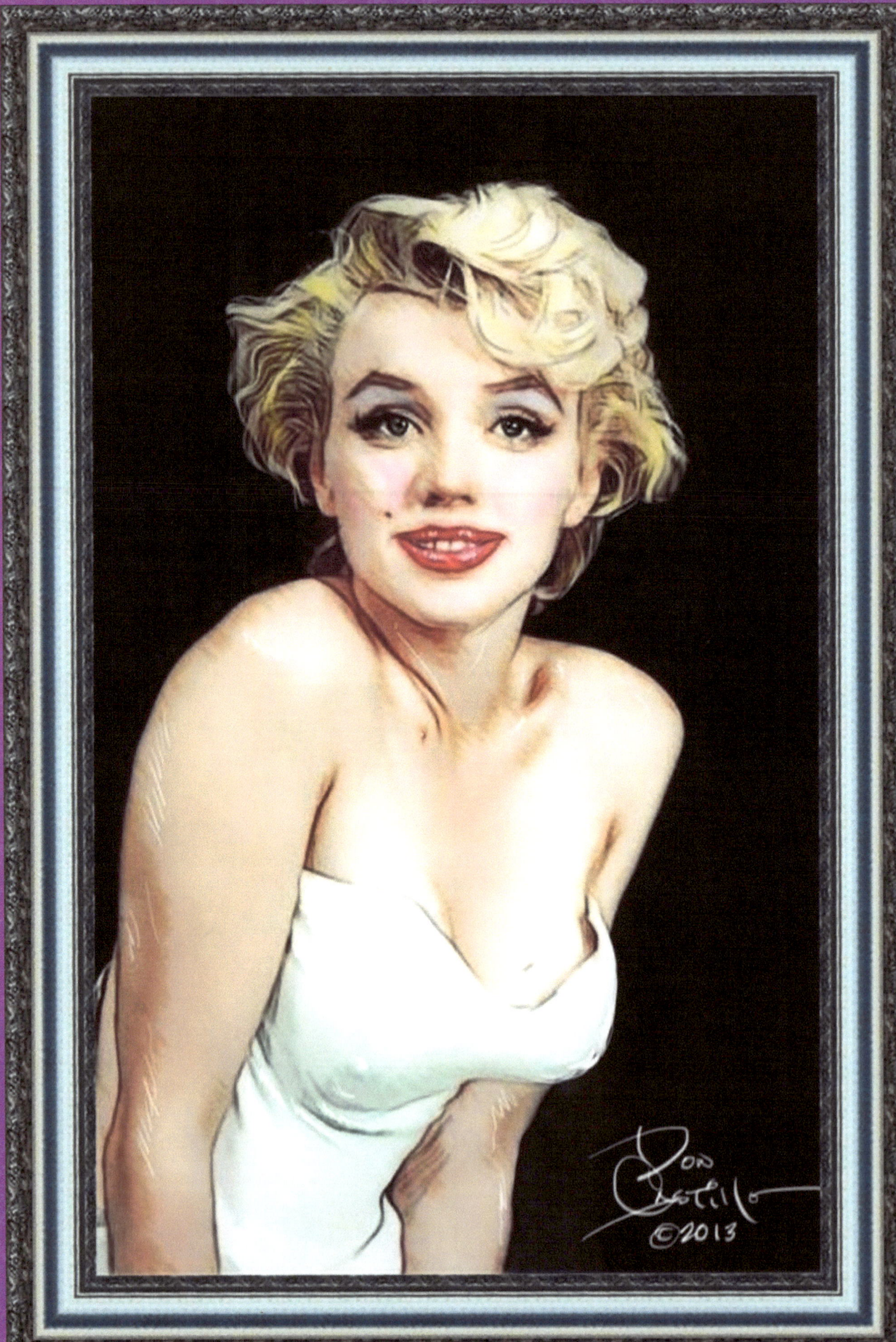

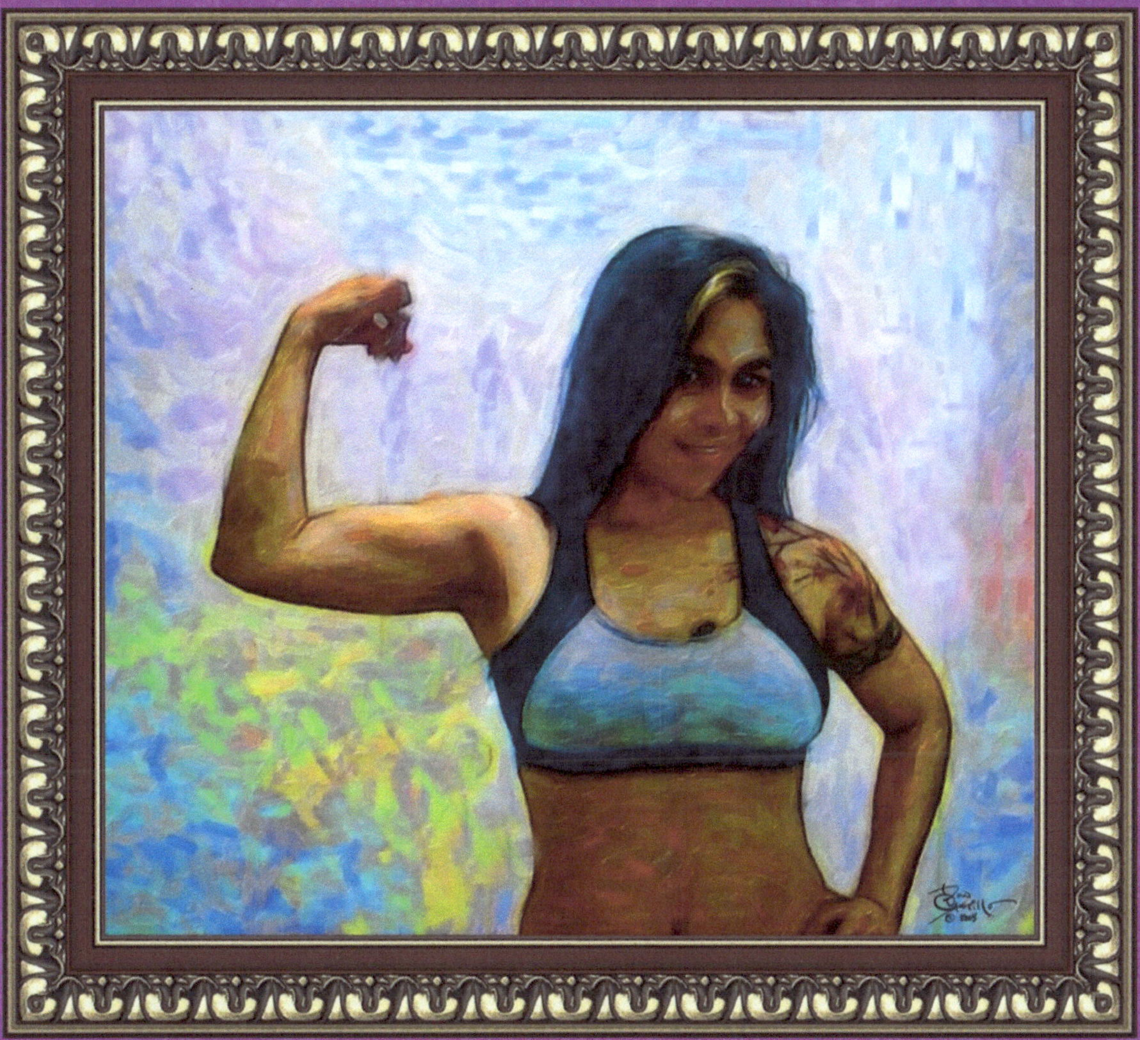

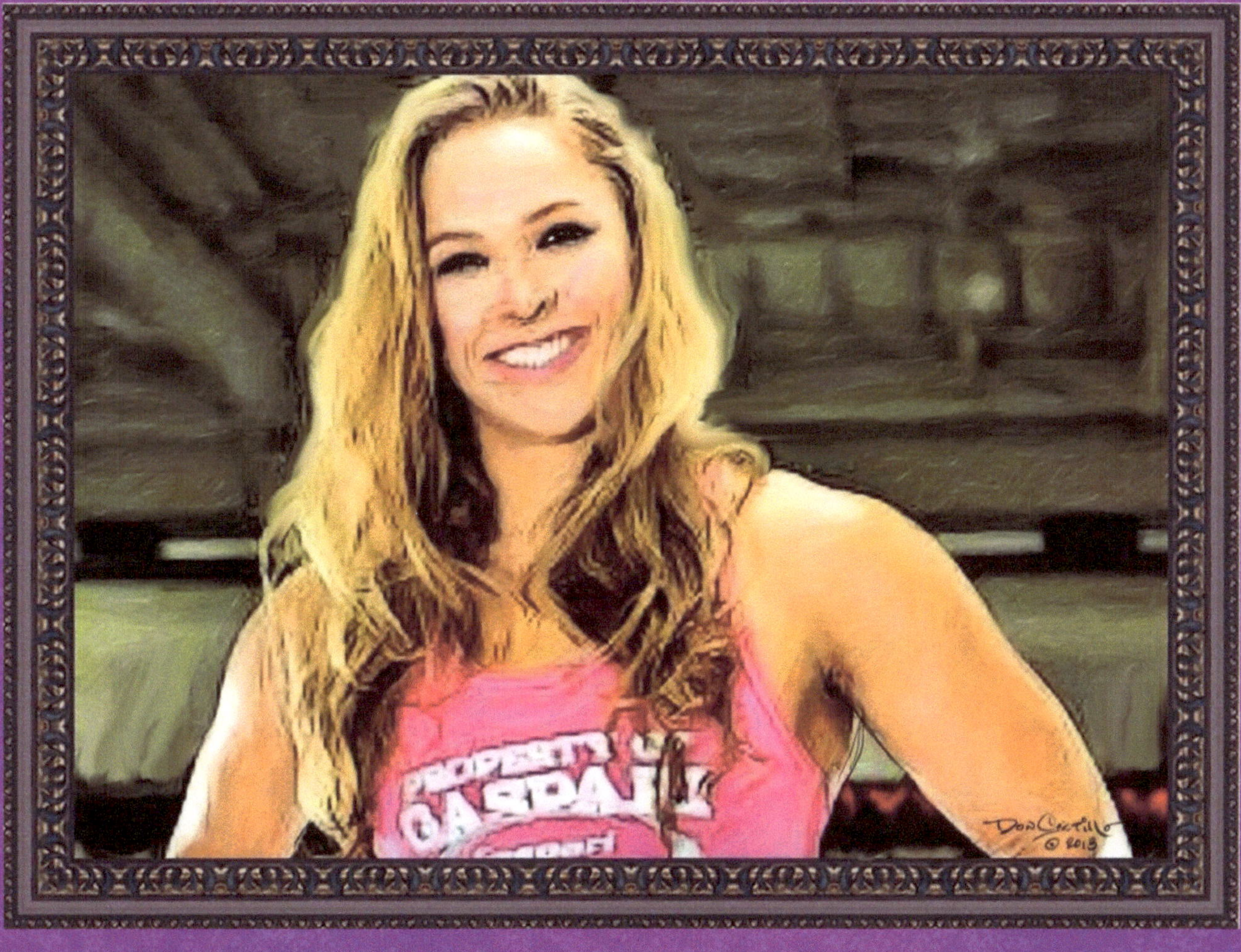

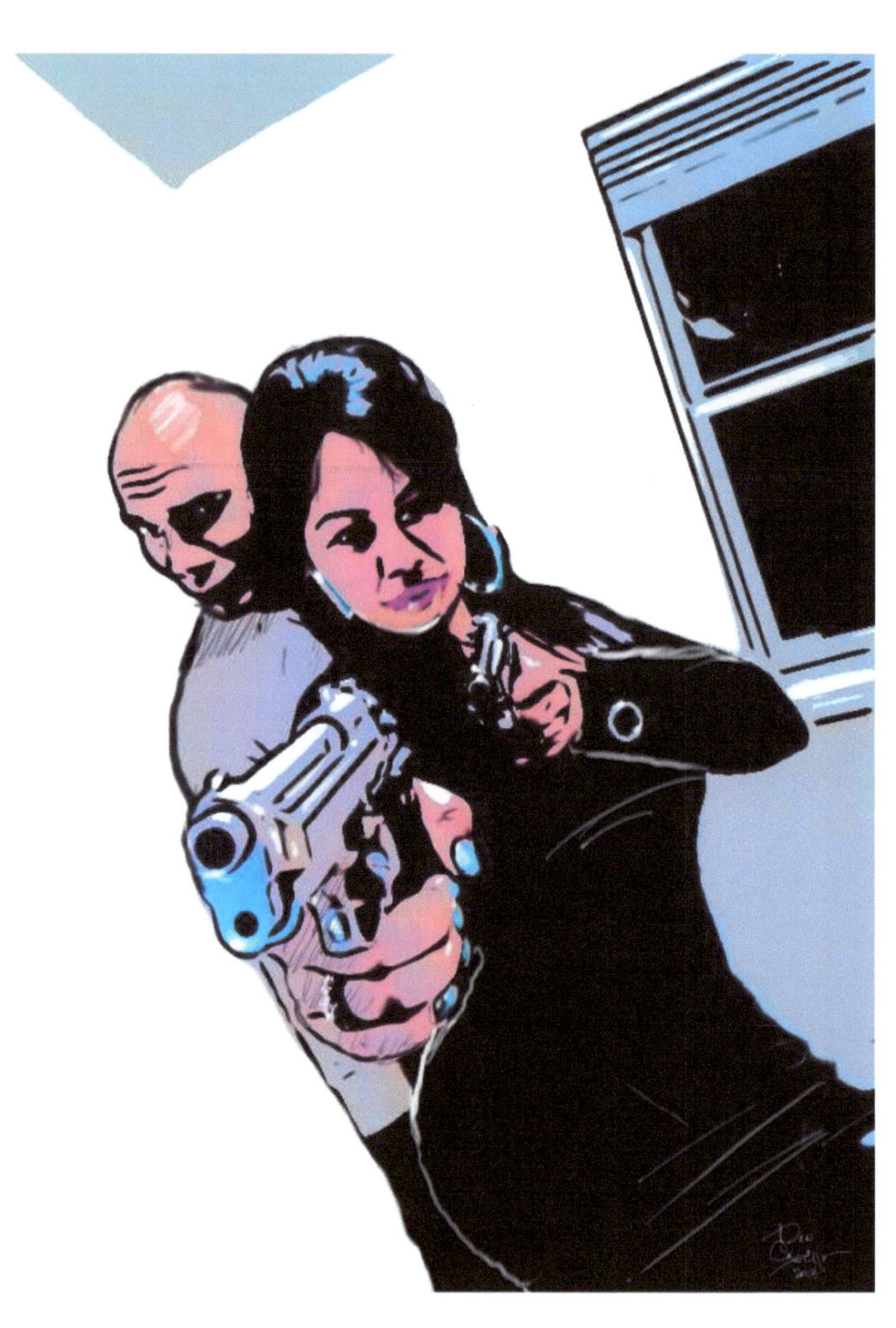

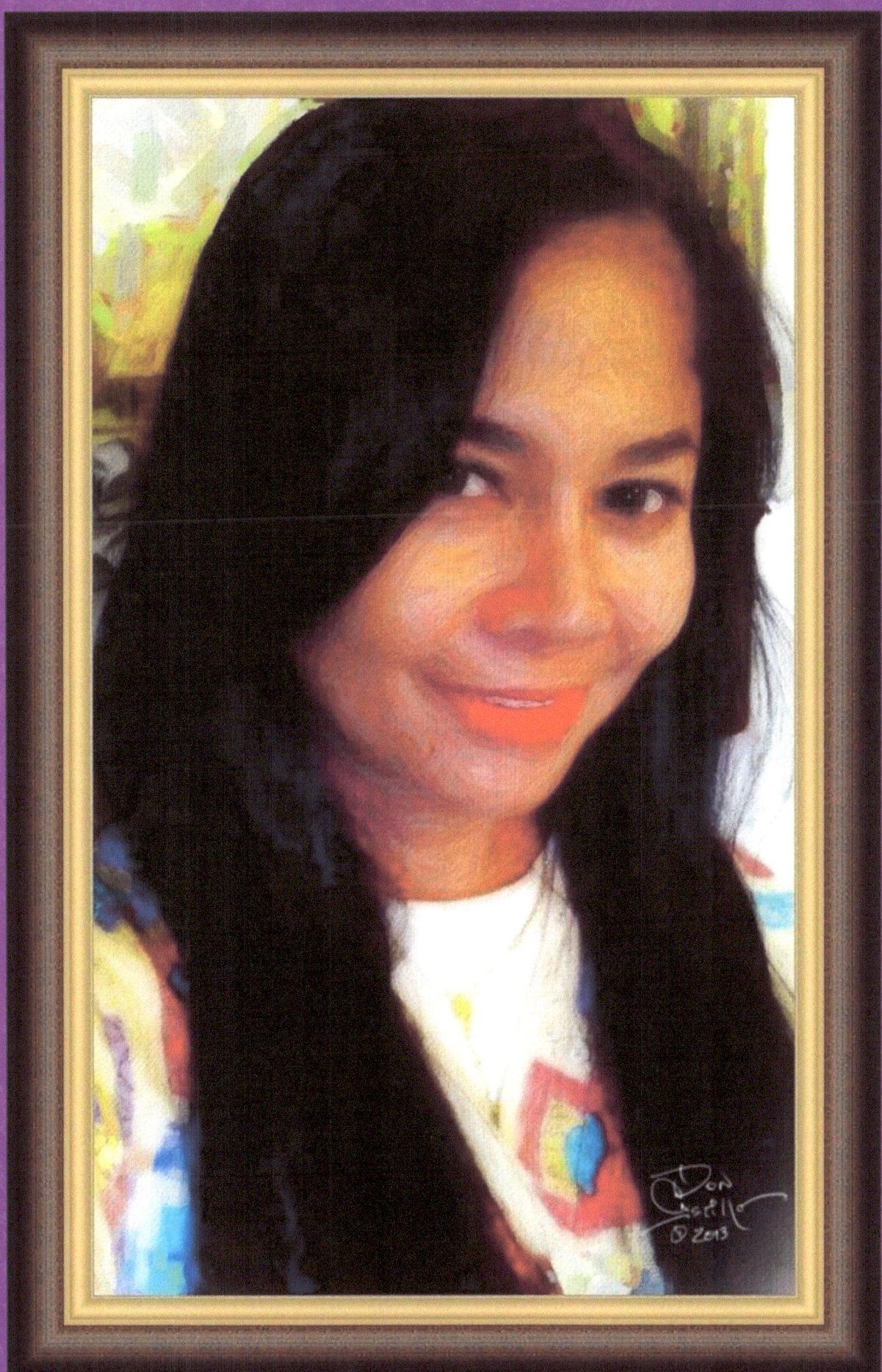

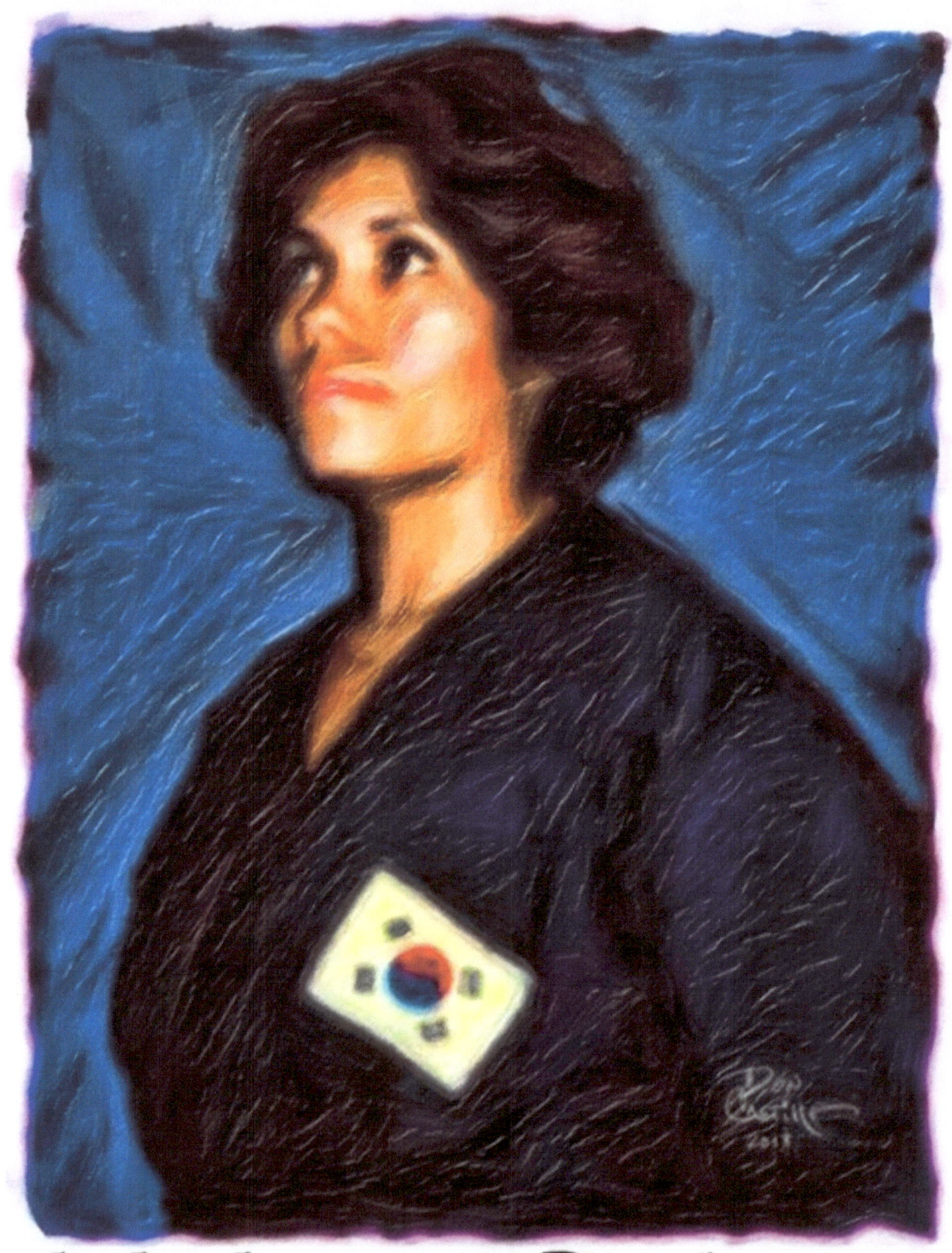

LULU LOURDES REA LOPEZ

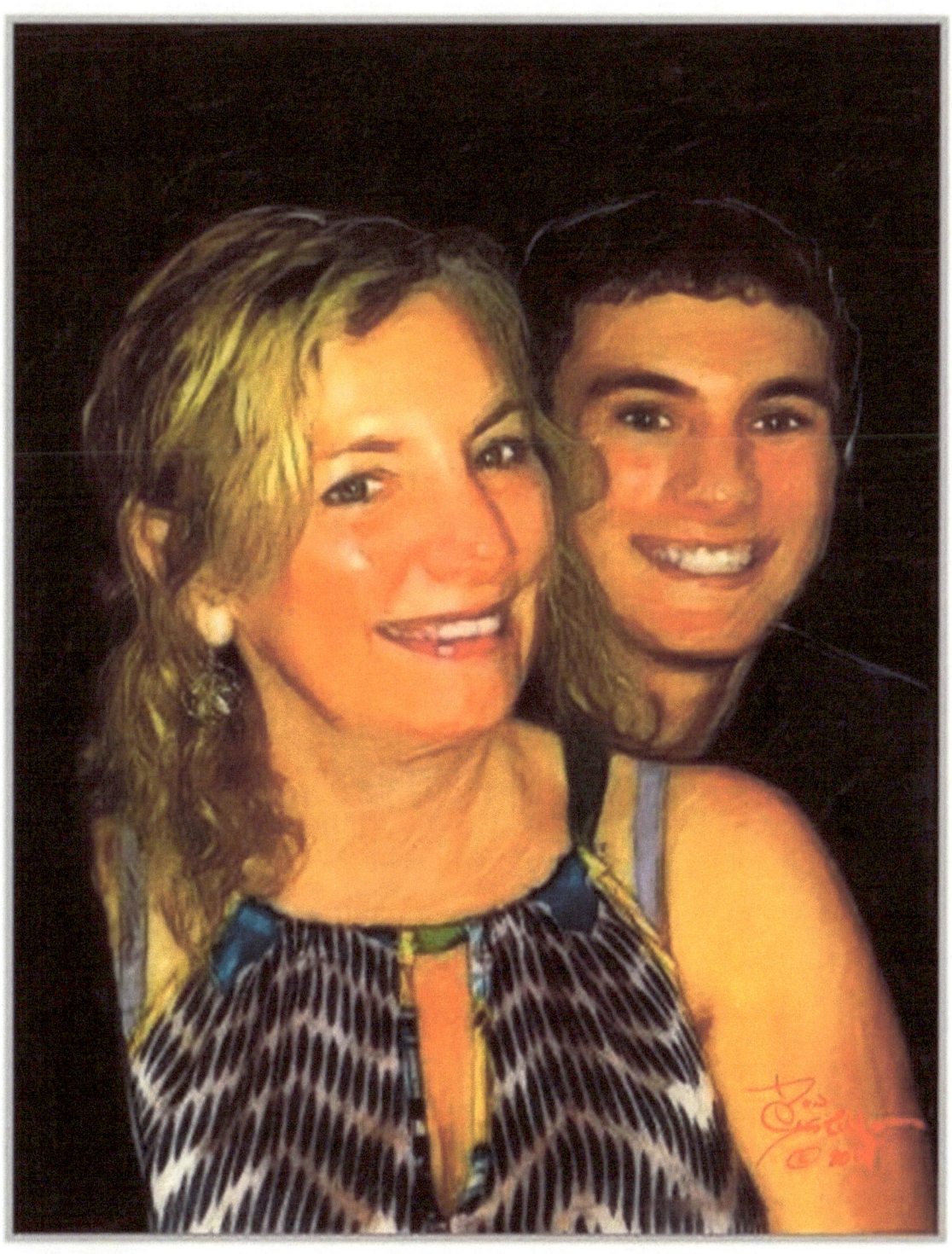

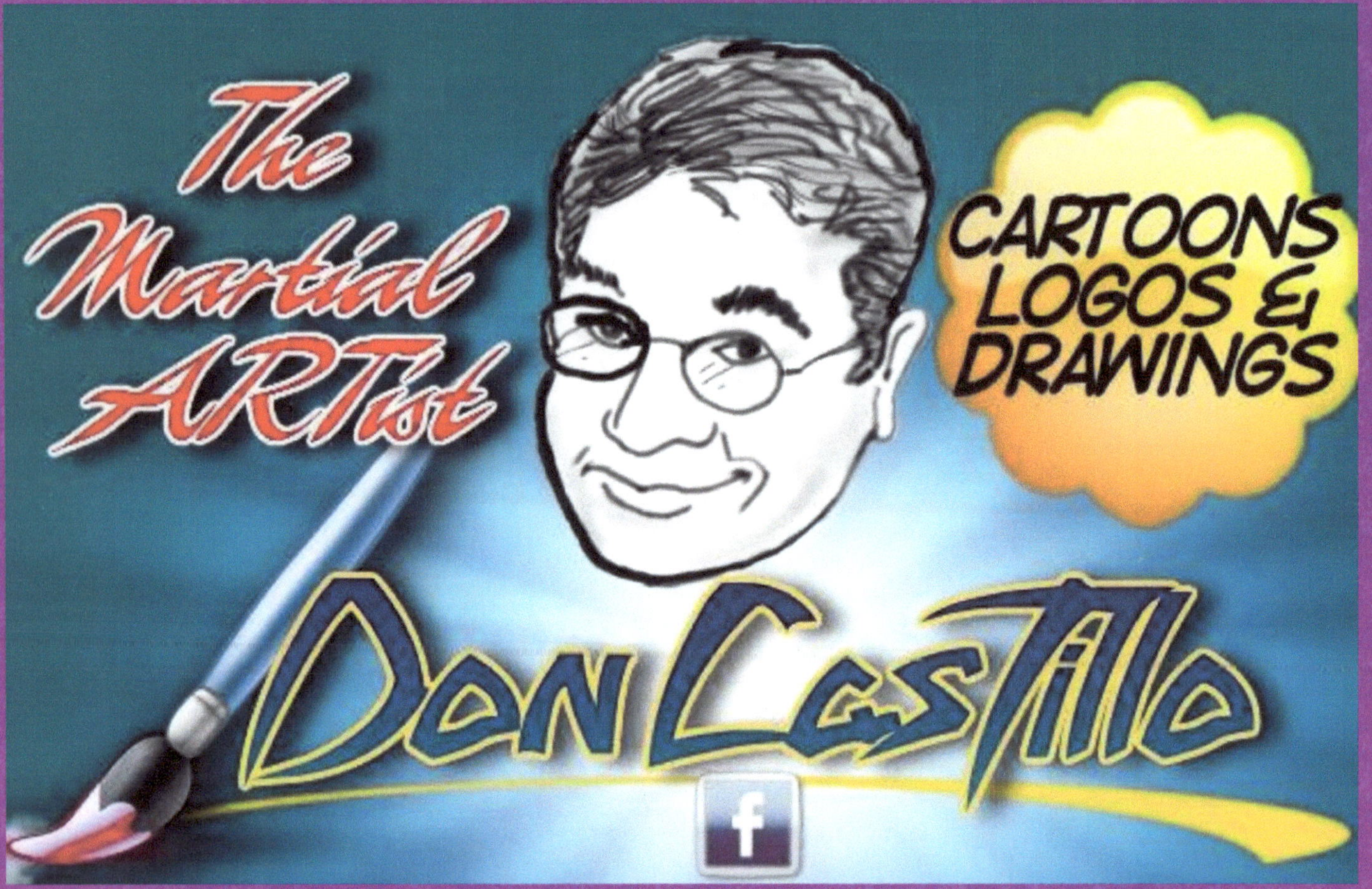

The Martial ARTist

CARTOONS LOGOS & DRAWINGS

Don Castillo

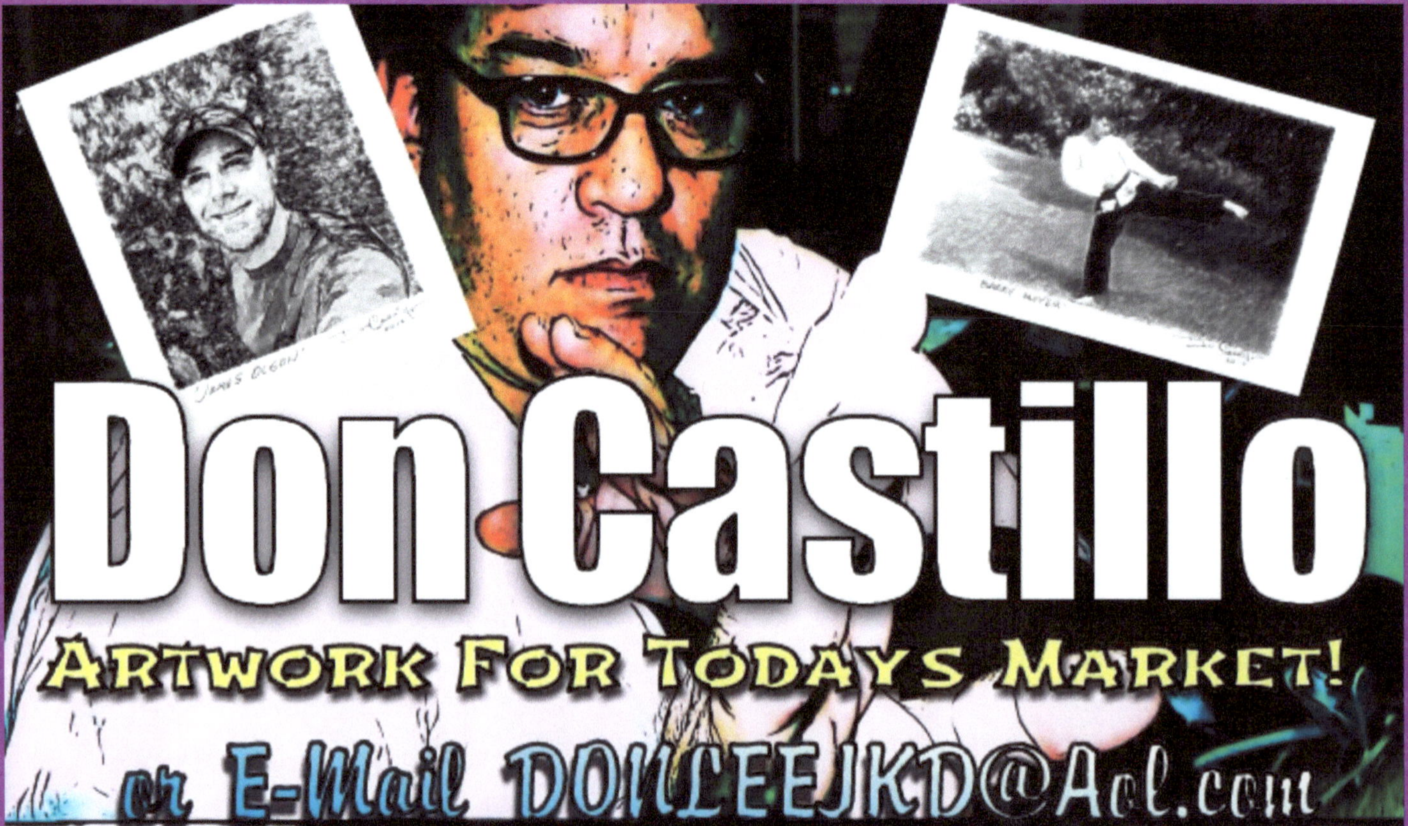

Don Castillo

Artwork For Todays Market!

or E-Mail DONLEEJKD@Aol.com

I WOULD LIKE TO DEDICATE
THIS BOOK TO:
MY WIFE TAMMY
AND ALL MY FAMILY
FOR STANDING BY ME
AS I SPENT MANY SLEEPLESS
NIGHTS WORKING ON THIS
BOOK, TO MY DAUGHTER
JILLIANNE LEE CASTILLO
FOR GIVING ME INSPIRATION
TO KEEP GOING, AND TO ALL
MY FRIENDS ON FACEBOOK
AND THE WORLD OVER FOR
SUPPORTING ME,
'THE MARTIAL ARTIST'

THANKS,
DON CASTILLO
LOVE YOU ALL!
FIND ME AT
DON CASTILLO
ON FACEBOOK
OR
DONLEEJKD@AOL.COM

PLEASE LOOK FOR
ALL MY BOOKS
AVAILABLE ON
AMAZON.COM